Cocktails in Color

Cocktails in Color

A SPIRITED GUIDE to the ART and JOY of DRINKMAKING

SAMMI KATZ & OLIVIA McGIFF

UNION
SQUARE
& CO.

NEW YORK

Liquid gold
(page 164)

Syrup made 3/23

Contents

Basil

Sage

Rosemary

Introduction

The first cocktail I ever remember falling in love with was the Honey Nut Old Fashioned from a long-gone New York City bar called JBird. I was a college freshman home on winter break, armed with a fake ID (sorry, Mom) and an incredibly impressionable mind. Somehow I charmed my way into one of JBird's sleek leather booths and ordered the drink I thought sounded the most sophisticated. The Honey Nut Old Fashioned, if I recall correctly, was incredibly simple: peanut-infused bourbon, honey syrup, and bitters. I don't think I'd even had a regular Old Fashioned at that point (I probably hadn't had ANY good cocktails at that point, let's be real), but the combination of flavors in the Honey Nut Old Fashioned was unlike anything I'd experienced before. It tasted like peanut brittle mixed with Honey Nut Cheerios® in drink form! It was wild! Perfectly cold, velvety, nutty, subtly sweet, slightly biting—it opened my eyes to the idea that cocktails are delicious blends of different tastes and flavors. They're also fun and a canvas for creativity, which is exactly how I feel about cooking and food.

Olivia and I met in a student theater group in college. We were both drama majors, and we spent four years making theater together—rolling on the floor, building sets, speaking in ridiculous accents. After every play's run was over, we would celebrate with a well-deserved drink. Sometimes that was a lukewarm can of Rolling Rock in a dorm room; sometimes it was an overly salted Margarita at the bar right off campus. Even if the drink itself was mediocre (which it most definitely was), it always felt joyous.

Throughout our post-grad endeavors and beyond, we would still regularly get together over food and drinks. We cooked and made cocktails in one of our small Brooklyn kitchens, appreciating and enjoying the simple,

pairings we liked and mixed 'em up, listening to what our palates were telling us, learning more with each sip. It was like experiencing the Honey Nut Old Fashioned again and again, but with different tastes every time. This practice and love continued to grow and evolve, so much so that we both gave our dogs spirit-related names (Juniper is Olivia's; Sherry is mine).

yummy things in life while we were figuring out the rest of it.

As I got more into bartending, I started inventing my own cocktails, and Olivia was my trusted taste tester. Since we're both foodies, we talked about making and tasting drinks the way we did cooking: in an ingredient-focused way centered on flavor. We looked at spirits and liqueurs as just ingredients on a shelf. Goslings rum tastes like burnt sugar, Campari is orangey, blanco tequila can be grassy. We'd find flavor

Olivia was delving into her career as an artist and would often paint portraits of my original cocktails. Her vibrant paintings matched the

more fun when shared with friends

playful nature of the cocktails I liked to make. The rich, creamy colors brought the drinks to life, making them feel approachable and joyful—the paintings were as delicious as the cocktails themselves! My experience behind the bar and her expertise sitting at the bar allowed our two perspectives to come together. It's how we have continued our collaboration over these ten years, sharing and combining our creative passions.

And now we're sharing them with you! This book is the tangible equivalent of hanging out with your bartender friend over drinks and getting to pick their brain about all things cocktails. I firmly believe that anyone should feel free to enjoy spirits and cocktails and make them their own; it shouldn't feel like an intimidating private club where you gotta know a guy who knows a guy. You don't need to come in with any prior knowledge of spirits. You don't need to have a "sophisticated palate." If you didn't know bourbon was whiskey until you just read this sentence, that's okay! This is a judgment-free zone!

Cocktails in Color celebrates the craft and joy of drinkmaking, from understanding the ingredients that comprise cocktails to shaking up and enjoying the delectable finished libations. With this book, we want to share our love of drinks and demystify the universe of cocktails to make it accessible. Cocktailing doesn't have to be this serious, uptight thing where men wearing vests are the gatekeepers of liquor and knowledge. How boring. So let's go on a journey through this boozy wonderland to give you the tools and confidence to create your own original cocktails. Here's the plan:

The first section is all about the *Spirits* you use to make cocktails. Here we break down the most important categories of spirits and their liqueur buddies, including how they're made and categorized, as well as some favorite bottles and flavor pairings.

Next is **Classic Cocktails.** I go over some basic cocktail rules you should know before diving in, then we look at 30 of the most foundational cocktails, the ones that are often used as building blocks when inventing other drinks. If there was a cocktail hall of fame, these babies would be the first class of inductees.

From there, we move on to *Original Cocktails.* I walk you through my tried-and-true methods for inventing your own drinks. (It's most certainly not how every bartender comes up with new cocktails, but it's how I do it. And that's good enough for me.) I explore these strategies further through a collection of original drink recipes I've created over the years, each harking back to one of the classics. They respect their elders but live their own lives, y'know? I'm also not interested in giving you a book of recipes that require you to buy or make something new for each drink. That's

exhausting on all fronts. So I've whittled the homemade ingredients and specialty liqueurs down to what I think are a manageable amount.

And finally, because I'd never leave you ill-prepared to take all this on, there's the **Bartending Index,** where you'll find the tools and techniques you need to execute all of the drinks in the book.

You can read *Cocktails in Color* cover to cover or skip around to sections you're interested in. Put it on your coffee table or your cookbook shelf. Get the pages a little stained from your cocktail experiments. If you feel slightly more self-assured next time you order a drink at a bar, I'll consider it a win. If you become the cocktail connoisseur of your friend group, congrats and enjoy not having to make small talk at parties. And if all this book does is make you smile, then we've done our job.

Spirits

GiN

↗ Juniper
the
Berry

Gin is my favorite spirit (but don't tell whiskey). That's because it's incredibly versatile, not just in how it's used but how it tastes. Gin starts as a neutral base spirit, then it's distilled with juniper.* Other botanicals often get thrown into the mix, and these can really be anything, from orange peel to anise to rose to cocoa. One gin can taste completely different than the next because of the botanicals used in distillation. Gin is bold enough to be the star in spirit-forward, stirred drinks like the classic Martini, and dainty enough to shine in refreshing, shaken cocktails like the incomparable Gimlet.

To pair flavors with gin, look at the botanicals used in the gin's distillation. What goes with those botanicals? Gin enjoys hanging out with fresh produce (berries, orange, grapefruit, celery) as well as fresh herbs! Try basil, rosemary, sage, cilantro. It also plays well with sparkling wine, orange liqueur, and fruit brandies. The possibilities are nearly endless.

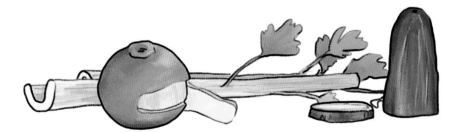

Keep 'em fresh!

So if you think you don't like gin, you probably just haven't had it the way you'd enjoy it the most. You know how long it took me to realize it was TONIC I didn't like and not gin? A really long time. Like, embarrassingly long.

*Not to be confused with Olivia's dog of the same name, juniper, specifically juniper berries, are the seed cones of certain juniper plants, which are a kind of evergreen shrub or tree. If you've ever thought that gin smells like a Christmas tree, that's juniper for you.

Juniper the Dog

Styles

London Dry:
The most common type of gin. Crisp, clean, and tasting primarily of juniper and citrus. It's perfect for pretty much any cocktail application.

Plymouth:
A smooth, earthy gin that, until recently, had to be made in Plymouth, England. There's really only one brand of Plymouth gin on the market today . . . called Plymouth.

Old Tom:
An old-school kind of gin, and not just because it's got "old" in the name. Traditionally, it's sweetened with sugar and/or other naturally sweet botanicals. A cross between London dry and genever.

Genever:
The original gin. The Dutch were the first to infuse neutral grain spirit with juniper; they called it "genever." It's distilled from a malted wine base, then redistilled with botanicals, so it's sweeter, richer, and maltier than other styles. It's the closest a gin will ever get to being a whiskey.

Navy Strength:
The no-joke gin. Similar to a London dry but packs an ABV (alcohol by volume) of 57%, compared to London dry's 45%.

Wild Card (also called New Style, New Wave, or International):
The gins that color outside the lines. They focus less on juniper and more on other botanicals. This is where gin really gets fun. (By the way, "wild card" is my name for them, so if you go somewhere and ask for a "wild card gin," you'll probably get just blank stares.)

Favorite Bottles

Tanqueray: A quintessential London dry gin. It can pretty much be paired with anything. Piney and herbaceous. It's the gin that's got your back.

Bols Genever: Aged, malt-forward, a little woodsy. Good for drinks where you might want to use a whiskey but feel like mixing it up.

Hayman's Old Tom: Soft, lightly sweet, tastes kind of like a candied orange peel. Perfect for adding body to a gin cocktail, like a Tom Collins or Martinez.

Perry's Tot: Distilled in New York, this bold, spicy, navy-strength gin isn't messing around. Somehow it's still super mixable, even if it can knock you over.

Hendrick's: I consider this a "wild card" gin. With notes of rose and cucumber, it's an excellent floral gin. My choice for Gimlets or any cocktail with fruits or veg.

VODKA

Okay, I've gotta be honest. Vodka isn't really my jam. By definition, vodka is a neutral grain spirit, the operative word here being neutral. It doesn't provide much of its own flavor. That being said, it's one of the most popular liquors in the whole dang world, so clearly, I'm in the minority.

Now produced globally, vodka originated in Eastern Europe. It's most often made from grains or potatoes, but any fermentable plant or fruit will do. It's first distilled to a crazy-high proof, then watered down to be drinkable. Since it's basically a blank canvas, vodka is perfect for making things like infusions and tinctures. (Unfortunately, this is also why flavored vodkas are so common. I recommend making yummy cocktails with a good bottle of unflavored vodka and leaving the cotton-candy-flavored one on the shelf.)

A vodka cocktail is gonna be all about the other ingredients in the drink; it sucks up flavor—kind of like tofu! Because neutrality is the name of vodka's game, it can take on big bold flavors like beets, licorice, lavender, and rose. It's also a great base spirit to showcase fruits like mango, pineapple, strawberries, and grapefruit. Get the veg involved, too, with carrots, cucumber, celery, and, necessary for a Bloody Mary, tomato!

This is also a great time to talk about vodka's cousin aquavit, a Scandinavian spirit that starts with a neutral base and is then infused with herbs and botanicals (but not juniper, so it's NOT gin), most commonly caraway, dill, anise, and fennel. It gives off some savory, licorice-y vibes.

Ketel One: Dutch vodka made from European wheat. Fairly clean and smooth.

Grey Goose: You have probably at least heard of this one or will recognize its frosted bottle. It's French, distilled from wheat, and generally considered a go-to vodka.

Tito's: People go nuts for Tito's. I once worked at a bar that didn't carry Tito's, and I've never received so many death glares before or since. It's made in Texas from corn, so it's got some of that subtle corn sweetness going on.

Aalborg Aquavit: Classic Danish aquavit that kind of tastes like rye bread.

Admittedly, not a whole lot of color in the vodka bottle world

RUM

Rum is not just for frozen piña coladas on a beach in the tropics (although sign me up for that any day). There's a whole universe of rums and rum cocktails out there to explore; in fact it's one of, if not THE largest and most diverse categories of spirit in the world! All rums have one thing in common: they're made from sugarcane or its by-products. That's it! That's all it takes to be a rum!

This amazing spirit has such a rough and complicated history that there's no way I could include everything about it in these few pages. Classifying rum is a tricky task. The most common shorthand for describing rum—as Spanish-, English-, or French-style—is rooted in colonialism, which is why many people are moving away from this classification system and instead categorize rum based on how or where it's made. Rum can be distilled from molasses (a by-product of the sugar-refining process) or fresh-pressed sugarcane juice. It's produced in many islands of the Caribbean, such as Puerto Rico, Cuba, Barbados, and Martinique, as well as in Indonesia, the Philippines, the United States, and a lot of other countries. Another simple way of categorizing rum is by how long it is aged: light or white for unaged or lightly aged rums, and dark or aged for rums that have spent quality time in a barrel.

Rum is incredibly versatile and fun to play with, once you get to know it. But there's still a terrible misconceived notion of what rum drinks are like that we need to debunk immediately.

(If, when I say rum, you think of Malibu, guess what? It's actually a liqueur, not even technically rum! No matter what Kevin from the lacrosse team says.) However, I will advise you to steer clear of spiced rum and artificially flavored rum, both of which are generally avoided by bartenders (and by me, after one terrible night when I was 18). Those rums are NOT GOOD, and other delicious rums shouldn't be punished for the sins of their peers.

You don't need a blender, artificial colors or sweeteners, or a 7-Eleven slushy machine to make an amazing rum cocktail. A Daiquiri, traditionally just white rum, lime, and sugar, is perfectly refreshing and balanced. An Old Fashioned made with dark aged rum is rich and satiny. Make your rum cocktails with fresh ingredients, serve them in real glassware made of glass— not plastic—and your views on rum will be forever changed. I promise.

There's no better example of the old saying that "what grows together goes together" than rum and its flavor pals. Because so much rum comes from the Caribbean, reach for tropical fruits like guava, passion fruit, pineapple, coconut, bananas, oranges. Rum's sweetness is a great counterpoint to spices like allspice, nutmeg, and ginger. And because it's aged in oak, dark rum loves rolling around with things like plums, nuts, chocolate, vanilla, and maple.

This spirit is extra special for cocktailing because rum loves to play with others in the sandbox. Meaning, a cocktail is often improved by using two or three different styles of rums instead of just one. Rum easily gets the award for best ensemble cast.

Bananas

Banana leaves

Styles

Light rum:

Also called silver or white rum. Most are unaged, but some may be matured in oak for a bit. It's relatively mild and sweet in flavor, so it's perfect for refreshing, shaken cocktails. If you've had a Mojito, you've had light rum.

Jamaican rum:

Super funky and distinct, it's full flavored and pungent, kind of like an overripe banana.

Dark rum:

Often distilled from molasses and aged in oak barrels. Rich and smooth, it's great in both shaken and stirred libations. Some dark rums taste like whiskey if you close your eyes.

Rhum agricole:

A type of rum mainly from Martinique and Guadeloupe. It's made from fresh-pressed sugarcane juice rather than molasses, making it grassy and earthy. (And the inclusion of the h in the word rhum isn't a typo; it signifies that it was made in a French-speaking country.)

Cachaça ("ka-SHA-sa"):

Brazilian sugarcane rum. It's only distilled once, so it's lower proof than some other rums. Soft and sweet, it can be aged or not. It's the only spirit to use in a Caipirinha.

Favorite Bottles

The Real McCoy 3 year white rum

A light rum from Barbados made in a sustainable distillery! Smooth, crisp, and floral, it's a great choice for Daiquiris or any shaken rum drink.

Bacardi Superior silver rum

Your most common and reliable light rum from Puerto Rico. If you're at a bar and don't see any other rums you recognize, chances are they'll have this.

Goslings Black Seal Rum — The only rum for a Dark 'n Stormy. From Bermuda, it's deep, syrupy, and downright yummy.

Cruzan Black Strap Rum — A dark rum made in the U.S. Virgin Islands. It's rich and caramelly, great to add a pinch of big flavor to a cocktail.

Rhum Barbancourt 8-year — An aged rhum agricole from Haiti that makes a stupid-good Old Fashioned.

Smith & Cross — A strong, earthy Jamaican rum that clocks in at 57% ABV (alcohol by volume). Drinks almost like a Scotch. For a flavor bomb, use it in a Negroni.

Avuá Amburana — A cachaça aged in indigenous amburana (or umbu-rana) wood, giving it a warm cinnamon note, but it's also juicy and spicy.

TEQUILA
& MEZCAL

Took one too many terrible tequila shots right after you turned 21? Same. Well, those shots were definitely BAD tequila, and you shouldn't let them deter you from enjoying delicious, beautifully made agave spirits. Unlike rum, which has no geographical restrictions and can be made anywhere in the world, tequila and mezcal must be made in Mexico. Tequila is distilled in the state of Jalisco and tends to be vegetal and bright; mezcal comes mainly from Oaxaca and is smoky and complex. And while mezcal can be made from a variety of agave species (of which there are around 200), tequila can ONLY be made from Blue Weber agave. What makes mezcal distinct is that the agave hearts are roasted underground in an earthen or stone pit before distillation, giving it its characteristic smokiness.

Agave spirits are famously great in mixed drinks (the Margarita has got to be one of the world's most beloved cocktails), but tequila's popularity outside of Mexico didn't boom until the mid-twentieth century. Though mezcal has been distilled in Mexico for centuries (like, since AT LEAST the sixteenth century), it's only been readily available in the U.S. since the 2000s, and it has become crazy popular within the last decade. And while it's great that this amazing spirit is getting the attention it rightly deserves, this increased appetite has put extreme stress on agave farmers, the species as a whole, and Mexico's ecosystem. Agave takes a long time to grow (seven years and upward), so the supply is struggling to keep up with the new demand.

Both tequila and mezcal love lime but also bright fruit like grapefruit, mango, watermelon, and raspberries. Take them in a more savory direction with things like tomatillos or flavors that are earthy and grassy, like turmeric or cumin. Often the downfall of some mezcal cocktails is they can be overwhelmingly smoky, so balance out that smoke with ingredients like honey, or get punchy with some ginger or chile peppers.

Very important: Only drink tequila and mezcal made from 100% agave. Some cheaper tequilas are made with half agave, half other added sugars. This is to cut down costs, but it also cuts down the quality. Splurge a little bit on the good stuff and you will be rewarded. Any cocktail bar worth its salt rim stocks only 100% agave tequila.

Types of Tequila

Blanco:

Also called Plata, silver, white, or platinum, it's not aged at all. Its brightness pairs really well with citrus, so it tends to be the best kind for shaken cocktails.

Reposado:

Aged in oak barrels between 2 and 12 months. It offers the brightness of a blanco, but it's a little softer around the edges. Delicious in a spirit-forward drink or on its own.

Añejo:

Aged in oak barrels between one and three years. It's the best sipping tequila, as the maturation makes it smoother and richer than others.

Extra Añejo:

Aged in oak barrels for at least three years. For when you wanna be extra.

TYPES of MEZCAL

Blanco/Joven (young):

Unaged and clear. Most mezcals are blancos. Great for both cocktails and sipping.

Reposado/Madurado (matured):

Like reposado tequila, it's aged in oak barrels between 2 and 12 months. Silky and delectable.

Añejo/Añejado (aged):

Aged in oak barrels for at least a year. I've never had one because they're pretty rare in the U.S., and if I've seen one on the shelves, it costs more than my rent.

Favorite Bottles

Espolón blanco: A clean, crisp blanco tequila. An excellent base for Margaritas and other refreshing cocktails.

Herradura reposado: Smooth, sweet, and a little spicy with vanilla notes. Great for sipping or cocktailing.

Don Julio 1942: An iconic añejo tequila that's ordered by high rollers. It's truly glorious, so if you can get your hands on the stuff (or get a billionaire to order you some), you'll be like, whoa that's tequila??

Del Maguey Vida mezcal: Del Maguey is an incredible distillery with a wide array of mezcals. The Vida is your starter, made from the most common agave plant for mezcal: espadín. Briny, reasonably smoky, and a great mixer. Can't go wrong.

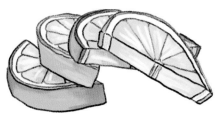

Banhez Tobalá mezcal: Tobalá is a wild agave varietal that can take up to 30 years to grow (!!), and it gives this mezcal a fresh green flavor with some citrusy notes. A perfect sipper to enjoy with some orange slices on the side, just like you're in a mezcalería in Oaxaca.

usually found on the top shelf

WHISK(E)Y

FOR a long time, whiskey has (wrongly) been considered a "man's drink," probably because of all the romanticized visions of cowboys swigging it in saloons and the patriarchal notion that women can't handle strong liquor. This is, of course, false. There is no such thing as a woman's drink or a man's drink. Anyone can like whiskey, and one of those people is me.

The world of whiskey is as vast as the Wild West, but two things all whiskies have in common are that they're distilled from grains and aged in oak barrels. Whiskey is made across the globe, and the type of grain used varies by region. It was one of the first spirits distilled in the U.S., so there are many drinks in the American cocktail canon with whiskey as the headliner.

And, all right, I've just gotta make sure it's clear: bourbon is whiskey, rye is whiskey, Scotch is whisky. They're all under the big, beautiful whiskey umbrella. If you want something sweet and smooth, try bourbon. Spicy and sharp? Go for rye. And if you want something smoky, hit up Scotch.

BOURBON

RYE

SCOTCH

Whiskey loves lemon but also other fruits like apples, oranges, peaches, and pears. It's friends with herbs like mint and rosemary, as well as sweeteners like honey and maple. The rich oakiness stands up to different nuts like peanuts and pecans, spices like cinnamon and ginger, and strong flavors like coffee and chocolate. With bourbon, play off the corn sweetness; with rye, balance out the spiciness; and with Scotch, have fun pairing with the smokiness.

You might also wonder why sometimes it's spelled "whiskey" versus "whisky." Next time you want to impress your friends and sound like a snob, tell them this: it's whiskey in Ireland and the U.S., and whisky in Scotland, Canada, and Japan. Why? I can't have ALL the answers.

pantry goodies

BOURBON

Goddess bless America for creating bourbon. Originally made in Kentucky, bourbon has to be at least 51% corn. It doesn't have to be made in Kentucky anymore, but it definitely has to be made in America. It also must be aged in new oak barrels for at least two years to be labeled "straight bourbon." Full, sweet, and velvety, it's awesome for both strong stirred drinks and lighter refreshing ones.

❧ FAVORITE BOTTLES ❧

Buffalo Trace Kentucky Straight Bourbon: Your best friend who's always there for you. Smooth, buttery, affordable. Drink it straight, in an Old Fashioned, or in a Whiskey Sour.

Four Roses Kentucky Straight Bourbon: Fruity and mellow with a lovely, honeyed sweetness. Great in all whiskey cocktails, but I especially love it in a Boulevardier.

Woodford Reserve Kentucky Straight Bourbon: I always have a bottle of this in my home bar. Perfect neat, on the rocks, or in a cocktail, it's floral, woodsy, and a great mid-shelf bourbon.

RYE

Rye whiskey has to be made from at least 51% rye grain. It also needs to be aged in oak barrels for at least two years to be considered "straight rye." Tangier and sharper than bourbon, it's similarly great in both stirred and shaken cocktails.

FAVORITE BOTTLES

Rittenhouse Bonded 100-Proof Kentucky Straight Rye Whiskey: Spiciness is front and center in this high-proof sucker, but it's still incredibly versatile. A good ol' workhorse rye. And it's one of only two rye whiskies to have survived Prohibition!

Michter's Kentucky Straight Rye: A soft and approachable rye with a spicy finish, kind of like a barista with a cute smile and killer tattoo sleeves. Delicious in a Manhattan.

Knob Creek Kentucky Straight Rye Whiskey: Bold and spicy with some nice herbaceousness. There's a lot of corn used in the distillation of this rye so it's awesome for bourbon drinkers who want to venture slightly outside their comfort zone.

the rye or die crew →

Scotch

Your dad's drink of choice. Made in Scotland (duh), Scotch is primarily distilled from malted barley and other grains, aged in bourbon barrels for at least three years, and smoky. A lot of Scotches get this smokiness from drying the grains over burning peat or partially decayed vegetation (yum). Single-malt Scotch is made from 100% malted barley and is generally for sipping. The flavor of the spirit is greatly influenced by where in Scotland it's distilled. Typically, the quality might be higher of an older single-malt (not always), but the price certainly will be. Blended Scotch is made from a blend of either two or more different single-malts, or a blend of single-malts and whiskies made from other grains.

⟨ FAVORITE BOTTLES ⟩

Monkey Shoulder Blended Malt Scotch Whisky: This guy blends single-
malts from three distilleries in Speyside to make a smooth, rich Scotch that's
perfect for mixing in a cocktail.

Laphroaig 10-year Islay Single-Malt Scotch: I learned the hard way
that this Scotch is pronounced "la-FROYG" and not the way I was butchering
it. This is the quintessential peaty Scotch
of your dreams if you love it, nightmares
if you hate it.

The Macallan 12-year Single-Malt
Scotch: Everyone likes Macallan. They have
so many different kinds and ages, it's a
great way to get into Scotch and learn
what you like. Though be careful—the
higher the age, the steeper the price
tag. So don't get cocky and order a
Macallan 30 if your wallet doesn't know
what it's in for.

SOME OTHER ONES!

IRISH WHISKEY

Also aged in bourbon barrels for at least three years. It has a smoother finish than Scotch.

CANADIAN WHISKY

Made from a blend of grains like corn and rye.

JAPANESE WHISKY

Comes in both blended and single-malt varieties, akin to Scotch.

TENNESSEE SOUR MASH WHISKEY

Lookin' at you, Jack Daniels.

AMERICAN SINGLE-MALT WHISKEY

A new breed of whiskey on the rise. Exactly what it sounds like: American whiskey made from a single grain.

31

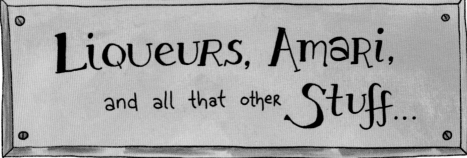

LIQUEURS, AMARI,
and all that other Stuff...

At this point, you've got the basics of the main spirits used in cocktails down. But what about everything else on cocktail menus that you frantically have to Google before your bartender asks you what you'd like? It's a big world out there. Let's make it a little more drinkable.

BRANDY

Brandy is a catchall term for any spirit distilled from fermented fruit juice. To pair flavors with brandy, think about what goes with the fruit from which the spirit is made. Lemon and orange are brandy's best friends. And because it's usually aged, brandy loves a good roll in the hay with flavors like chocolate, vanilla and coffee.

| Cognac | Grape brandy made in the Cognac region of France, aged at least two years in oak barrels, caramelly and spicy. |

| Pisco | Unaged grape brandy from Peru or Chile. Floral and citrusy. |

| American apple brandy | Also called straight apple brandy, it's like an aged, rich apple. |

| Calvados | French apple brandy made in the Calvados region of Normandy, it's got a crisp and funky flavor. |

| Eau-de-vie | Clear brandy distilled from the fermented juice of a fruit. Perfect for adding a bright, fresh flavor to a cocktail. |

LIQUEURS

Liqueurs are essentially spirits with added flavorings and sweeteners. They're a cocktail's support system—not always required, but whenever you text them, they're ready to join the party. There are many, many, MANY liqueurs out there. Here's a tiny sampling of the ones you'll encounter in this book and beyond.

Chartreuse ("shar-TRUCE") A French herbal liqueur made by monks, and only the monks know the recipe (seriously). It's got so much going on: it's smooth, it's spicy, it's sweet, it's kind of medicinal—but in a fun way! There are two main varieties: green (vert) is the quintessential one; yellow (jaune) is a bit milder and lower proof.

Triple sec A sweet orange-flavored liqueur used in a lot of classics. The usual suspects spotted at a bar are Combier, Cointreau, curaçao, and Grand Marnier (which is technically an orange brandy, but it's often used like a triple sec). They can be used interchangeably, for the most part.

Maraschino ("mare-uh-SKEE-no") Cherry-flavored liqueur that is light and delicate, also used in So. Many. Classics.

St-Germain An elderflower liqueur that comes in the prettiest bottle!

Campari A ubiquitous Italian liqueur that tastes like bitter orange and grapefruit. Essential to a classic Negroni.

Aperol Like Campari but sweeter and less intensely bitter.

Crème de mûre / crème de cassis Mûre is blackberry, cassis is black currant.
They're different, but if you can find only one and not the other, it won't kill ya.

Absinthe An overproof spirit (meaning it has a higher alcohol content than a standard spirit) that tastes of wormwood and anise. Use sparingly, in dashes or as a rinse (page 172), because it can be pretty overwhelming. And no, it will not make you hallucinate and see the green fairy, unless you consume mass quantities.

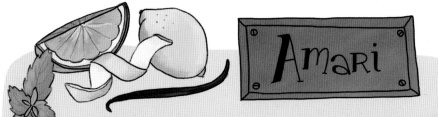

Amari

Amari (the plural of amaro) are bittersweet Italian liqueurs made of herbs, roots, and spices, traditionally served after a meal as a digestif. They add depth and complexity when used in cocktails, and there are a lot of them, each with its own identity and personality. Even though humans were initially wired to reject anything bitter because it could be poisonous, today bitter is not a bad thing. It's a taste just like any other, and Americans are learning to embrace it as something that can be totally delicious.

Italy invented amaro, but it can be produced anywhere. These are just A FEW of the amari that are out there. Find your favorites, and you'll want to sip them after dinner or start trying to find ways to add 'em into your cocktails.

Amaro Averna Bittersweet and viscous, with hints of chocolate and citrus.

Amaro Montenegro Made from 40 botanicals, it's slightly bitter and vanilla sweet, with hints of orange and grapefruit. I love this ingredient so much. In fact, my nickname behind the bar is Baby Monte, because my shot of choice is a tiny bit of Montenegro.

Cynar ("chee-NAR") An amaro that's made from artichoke, but it does NOT taste like an artichoke. It's citrusy and vegetal, giving a nice oomph to a cocktail.

Fernet-Branca As polarizing as an amaro, or really anything in the world, can get. There are folks who love it; others who despise it. I'm in the latter camp, but it's lauded by some for its medicinal and menthol-like quality. Often used as a Hello or Goodbye shot among bartender friends. (Give me my Baby Monte instead, thank you.)

Fortified Wines

Wait, what, isn't this a cocktail book? Yes, yes it is. But there are several fortified wines used as cocktail ingredients that we gotta get into. Fortifying a wine means adding a distilled spirit to it, thus increasing its alcohol content but also its flavor and its shelf life. Sherry is one of the most common fortified wines (and no, I'm not talking about your nana's super-sweet cooking sherry). There's also aromatized wine, which has been flavored with herbs and spices. This is where you'll find the Martini's best pal, vermouth.

The main pro tip about vermouth and other fortified wines is that they're fresh products, just like wine... because they're also wine. So please store them in the fridge once you've opened them, and know that they WILL turn on you (as in go bad, not become evil). If you're at a bar that has an open bottle of vermouth just hanging out on the back shelf, don't order a cocktail there. You're welcome.

Sherry & Port

Sherry is not just for Jewish grandmothers nor the name of my dog. It's fortified wine made in Spain, specifically the area around Jerez, and runs the gamut from being bone dry to super sweet. Sherry lends a lovely fruity, nutty quality to cocktails. Port is made in the Douro river valley in Portugal. It's best known as a dessert wine, but it can also be a great cocktail ingredient.

Fino and Manzanilla sherries	Dry white sherries that can be briny and acidic.
Amontillado & oloroso sherries	Darker than fino, lighter than cream sherries; nutty and aromatic.
Pedro Ximénez & cream sherries	The richer ones. Use sparingly; a little goes a long way.
Ruby port	Made from young red wine with bright fruit flavor.
Tawny port	Made by blending vintages of oak-aged wine, it tastes more like dried fruit.

Sherry the dog

Sherry the drink

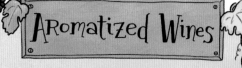

Aromatized Wines

These white wines have been fortified with a neutral spirit, then flavored with herbs and spices.

Dry vermouth
Pale, a little bitter, and, uh, dry. It's used in Martinis and generally gets along with lighter spirits like gin and vodka.

Sweet vermouth
Red, rich, and, yes, sweet. It's used in Manhattans and Negronis and tends to hang with darker spirits like whiskey.

Blanc vermouth
Sometimes called white or bianco vermouth, it's the middle ground between dry and sweet, and it is really good in cocktails. It plays well with both light and dark spirits. She's your trusty floater friend!

Lillet Blanc
A classic fortified wine made with citrus liqueur. It is floral and orangey and can be used like a blanc vermouth.

Cocchi Americano
Flavored with gentian root, orange, and spices. Slightly more bitter than Lillet, but it can still be used as an alternative.

Bitters

Think of bitters like a spice rack. They have their own flavor but also have an uncanny ability to tie together other ingredients. Bitters are neutral, high-proof spirits with loads of herbs, bark, spices, and roots added to them, and they are used as a flavoring agent in cocktails. Just a dash of a certain bitter can really alter the taste of a drink, and most of the time, you won't be able to identify what it is. They're like the mysterious stagehands who make the whole thing run smoothly, and you're like "How did you do that?" and they just shrug their shoulders and keep doing their job. The most common bitters are Angostura bitters (herbal and distinct), orange bitters (I love Regans'), and Peychaud's (sort of cherry and anise flavored), but you can now find flavors like grapefruit, lavender, cardamom, chocolate, celery, and tobacco. If you can name it, there's a bitters for it. Bitters are measured in dashes, either combined with the other ingredients before shaking or stirring or added on top of the finished drink as a garnish that adds some extra aromatics.

Classic
Cocktails

Understanding Classics

Before we dive headfirst into the recipes themselves, there are some fundamental rules to know. The cocktail world can be seen as inaccessible or confusing, but it really doesn't have to be! By learning a few classic cocktail templates, you'll understand more about how flavors pair and ingredients come together. Think about these templates like the "mother sauces" in cooking. According to the French (they do know a lot about food), there are just a handful of sauces you need to master in order to make all other sauces. Cocktails effectively work the same way! Once you get the basics under your belt, everything will feel a lot easier.

The key to each template, and any great cocktail, is BALANCE. In Samin Nosrat's incredible book on the foundations of cooking, "Salt, Fat, Acid, Heat," she says that the key to making a great dish is to find the balance among those four elements. With cocktails, the components are different, but the philosophy is the same. Find the right balance of flavors in a drink—strong, sweet, bitter, sour—and you will unlock its deliciousness.

Here's the thing: we're working on a really small scale! If all you're dealing with is 3 total ounces of liquid, everything has to be in harmony. Altering just ¼ ounce of an ingredient can radically change the way a cocktail tastes. It might seem totally ridiculous, but you'll notice a huge difference if you use only ½ ounce of simple syrup in a Daiquiri instead of ¾ ounce. It'll go from stupid delicious to super tart really fast. So it's important to get all of your ingredients in the right proportions.

When you flip through the recipes in this section, you'll find some of the same formulas repeating themselves over and over. Varying a cocktail's recipe just a little bit can transform it into a whole new drink. Add mint to a Gimlet and it's now a Southside. Make a Manhattan with Scotch, and it's a Rob Roy. Swap in honey syrup for simple in a Whiskey Sour, and suddenly it's a Gold Rush. See what I mean? (If these words still mean nothing to you, don't worry, hopefully they will soon.)

Essentially, there are two styles of cocktails: shaken and stirred.

SHAKEN COCKTAILS

Cocktail shaking is so much fun to do, and it engages all your senses. Shaking gives you that incredible moment when you step into a bar and are welcomed with the glorious sound of ice crackling against metal. Or the cold sensation of the tins getting frosty underneath your hands after a long day when you just want to feel SOMETHING. Okay, I'm going off the rails now.

Shaking is the most efficient way to chill and dilute a cocktail. But it also adds texture in the form of little, tiny air bubbles. That gorgeous citrus foam you see on top of a shaken drink when a bartender sets it down in front of you? Air bubbles, baby.

Any cocktail that contains texturizers such as citrus, fruit juice, eggs, or dairy should be shaken, not stirred. These cloudy ingredients need to be agitated in order to fully emulsify and integrate into the drink. (To learn how to shake a cocktail, turn to page 170.)

Generally, shaken cocktails are bright and refreshing, and the liquor is not necessarily the center of attention. An important way to amp up the deliciousness of a shaken cocktail: Please squeeze your own citrus rather than buying citrus juice! If it makes up one-third of your cocktail, you want it to be the best quality. And always taste your juice before shaking up a drink—lemons and limes vary in tartness, so one fruit might be more sour than the next.

Just one more thing: Sugar in a cocktail helps to sweeten it, yes, but it also adds body and serves as a binder for the rest of the ingredients. Don't ask for a cocktail to be made without sugar—it will be terrible. (Are you a nonbeliever? Make a Daiquiri without any simple syrup, then come talk to me.) If you really don't want any sugar at all, drink a vodka soda.

There are two main styles of shaken cocktails:

Sour-style cocktails are made of a base spirit, some form of citrus or acid, and some type of sweetener. Liquor, sour, sweet: the tripod of a sour-style cocktail. If one is out of whack, the whole thing falls over. These cocktails are perfect for cooling down on a hot day or for pretending you're somewhere else during a snowstorm. Most shaken cocktails are some kind of a sour.

Collins-style cocktails are essentially sours that are fizzy. They typically have a higher volume of liquid because of the addition of whatever bubbles you're using, whether it's seltzer, sparkling wine, or tonic. Basically, if it's carbonated and you add it to your drink, congratulations! Your cocktail is now Collins-style.

STIRRED COCKTAILS

I find stirring a cocktail to be really soothing. There's something so serene about that repetitive, quiet motion of swirling a barspoon around a mixing glass. Stirring requires more time and patience than shaking does. Less physical effort, more mental focus. I guess you could say stirring is for the book nerds and shaking is for the cool athletes. But I like to be a well-rounded student.

Stirring has two purposes: chilling and diluting a cocktail. Shaking does this, too, of course, but when you stir a cocktail, you avoid making air bubbles when you want the texture to be smooth, almost velvety. You should stir a cocktail that contains entirely transparent ingredients, like liquor, liqueurs, sweeteners, fortified wines, and bitters. These ingredients don't need to be rattled around in a tin in order to become incorporated, just gently coaxed until they come together. It takes a bit more time to get the cocktail to the right temperature and dilution point when you stir, but it's worth it when that first sip is so delightfully silky. Stirred cocktails tend to be spirit-forward and aromatic, with the flavors of the liquor front and center. (To learn how to stir a cocktail, turn to page 171.)

There are two main styles of stirred cocktails:

Old Fashioned-style cocktails are traditionally made up of a base spirit, a small amount of sugar, and bitters. The balance here comes from enhancing the flavor of your base spirit; you want to soften the edges and add complexity. You can think about an Old Fashioned-style cocktail like a steak dinner. Yeah, there are other components on the plate, but their purpose is to support the main star.

Martini-style cocktails are very similar to Old Fashioned-style ones, but a fortified wine and/or liqueur (a "modifier," in the biz) takes the place of the sweetener, and usually in larger amounts. (Manhattans and Negronis fall into this category.) You still want to find balance by enhancing the base spirit, rounding it out with a modifier, then adding a third component to bridge the gap between the two. A Martini-style cocktail is kind of like a bowl of chili: all the different ingredients work together to make up one delightful whole.

2 ounces bourbon

½ ounce demerara syrup (page 162)

3 dashes each Angostura and orange bitters

1 orange twist, for garnish

1 lemon twist, for garnish

Combine all the ingredients except for the garnishes in a rocks glass over one big ice cube and stir until chilled.

Garnish with the orange and lemon twists and serve.

Old Fashioned

The earliest mentions of the word *cocktail* define it as a combination of spirit, sugar, water, and bitters—which happens to be the recipe for the Old Fashioned, making this drink the grandmomma of all cocktails. Nothing is better than a perfect Old Fashioned. But perfect is subjective, depending on who is doing the drinking. Some purists prefer a simple mix of whiskey (either rye or bourbon works), simple syrup, and Angostura bitters. Others muddle oranges and/or cherries in the bottom of the glass. Still others use a sugar cube or demerara syrup instead of simple, several kinds of bitters, or even seltzer to top (which personally makes me cringe, but to each their own). I've found my favorite way to stir up this cocktail. That's the beauty of an Old Fashioned—you can make it entirely yours.

Martini

Like the Old Fashioned, the Martini is another example of a simple union (in this case, liquor and vermouth) that has stood the test of time. When I say "Martini," I'm not referring to those insane, highlighter-colored 'tinis of the 1990s. A true Martini is a fairly achromatic beauty. Its base recipe is pretty straightforward, but the fun lies in its customizability. You can't say, "I'll have a Martini" and leave it at that. There are so many follow-up questions! Gin or vodka? Dry or dirty, olives or a lemon twist, up or on the rocks? Gosh, Martinis require so many decisions. One question that's not worth asking, though, is "shaken or stirred?" Stir it. There are no fresh juices that require shaking; it's straight liquor! Stir. It.

As a bartender, I've found the most common order for a Martini these days is dry, meaning with a lower ratio of vermouth to spirit, but there are a lot of other ways to order a Martini, too. Try it with varying levels of vermouth, even going as far as a 50/50 split . . . just make sure your vermouth is fresh and hasn't been oxidizing in a cabinet for years. (I do draw the line at "extra dry," which essentially means no vermouth. If you ask me, that's not a cocktail; it's just cold alcohol.) So get some friends over, make a bunch of Martinis, and find what you like! Just remember to have some snacks around; you'll need 'em.

2½ ounces gin OR vodka

½ ounce dry vermouth

2 dashes orange bitters (optional)

3 olives skewered on a cocktail pick

OR 1 lemon twist, for garnish

Combine all the ingredients except for the garnish in a mixing glass filled with ice. Stir until chilled and strain into a Nick and Nora glass. Garnish with the olives or the lemon twist and serve.

VARIATIONS

50/50: Also known in the biz as "the bartender's Martini," use 1½ ounces gin and 1½ ounces dry vermouth.

Dirty: Decrease the gin or vodka to 2 ounces and add ½ ounce olive brine. Garnish with olives, obvi.

Gibson: Take your preferred Martini recipe and sub a pickled cocktail onion as garnish.

delicious up or on the rocks

2 ounces rye or bourbon

1 ounce sweet vermouth

3 dashes Angostura bitters

1 brandied cherry skewered on a cocktail pick, for garnish

Combine all the ingredients except for the garnish in a mixing glass filled with ice. Stir until chilled and strain into a Nick and Nora glass. Garnish with the cherry and serve.

MANHATTAN

Ah, Manhattan. My hometown and one of my favorite classic cocktails. Anytime I'm feeling a little down, I order a Manhattan. When the bartender sets it in front of me and I take the first sip, a wave of calm washes over me. Sipping on a good Manhattan is like sinking into an armchair that knows you well.

There's a lot of lore about where the Manhattan was invented. Probably at the Manhattan Club in the late 1800s, but maybe by some guy on the Lower East Side? Who's to say? That's the thing about cocktail history—it all took place in a bar, so no one can be trusted as a reliable narrator. Whoever it was, though, kudos and thank you.

You can use either rye or bourbon in your Manhattan. I prefer rye as I find its spiciness cuts through the sweetness of the vermouth.

VARIATIONS

Dry: Substitute dry vermouth for sweet and garnish with a lemon twist.

Perfect: Use ½ ounce dry vermouth and ½ ounce sweet vermouth. Garnish with a lemon twist.

Rob Roy: Just make your Manhattan with Scotch! Done.

Arguably the best Italian import besides burrata and Isabella Rossellini, the Negroni is a case study in flavor. First you've got the gin with all its fun botanicals; next the vermouth, which mellows out the gin and adds its own characteristics; then you've got the bing-bang-boom of Campari, which adds a punchy bitterness and even more herbs and fruit. It's a simple drink that has generated a whole category of variations. But if you're new to bitter cocktails, start with the team captain.

The traditional way to make a Negroni is to use equal parts of each ingredient, and that's a hill I was willing to die on . . . until I tried one made with two parts gin to one part each Campari and vermouth. It was like my world turned upside down, and I haven't gone back. I think the Campari is less overwhelming with the gin bumped up a bit, so I find the drink to be more balanced. Also don't let anyone ever shake it or serve it up, without ice. It's just wrong.

VARIATIONS

Americano: Combine 1 ounce Campari and 1 ounce sweet vermouth in an ice-filled Collins glass and top with seltzer. Garnish with an orange twist.

Sbagliato: Make an Americano but use Prosecco instead of seltzer! Sbagliato means "mistake" in Italian, but this drink tastes just right to me.

White Negroni, aka French Negroni: Use 1½ ounces gin, 1 ounce Lillet Blanc, and ½ ounce Suze and garnish with a lemon twist.

NEGRONI

1 ½ ounces gin

¾ ounce sweet vermouth

¾ ounce Campari

1 orange twist, for garnish

Combine all the ingredients except for the garnish in a
rocks glass over one big ice cube and stir until chilled.
Garnish with the orange twist and serve.

DAIQUIRI

Olivia's favorite

2 ounces white rum
¾ ounce lime juice
¾ ounce simple syrup
   (page 162)
1 lime wheel, for
   garnish (optional)

Combine all the ingredients except for
the garnish in a shaker tin filled with ice.

Shake until chilled, strain into a
Nick and Nora or coupe glass,
garnish with the lime wheel,
if desired, and serve.

I'm not talking about a Sandals Resort® frozen strawberry Daiquiri here. This is the traditional beauty, made of good rum, fresh lime juice, and simple syrup, shaken and served up. That's it. An expertly made Daiquiri is the perfect cocktail: it's bright, citrusy, beyond refreshing. When I don't know what I want to drink, I ALWAYS want a Daiquiri. It's almost too easy to throw back and just as easy to say, "I'll have another."

This is a great place to explore the wider category of rum. Different styles of rum love to play with each other, so experiment a bit. Add ¼ ounce of a funky Jamaican rum, or go equal parts white rum and rhum agricole. I personally don't garnish my Daiquiris, but if you want an extra bit of tartness, float a lime wheel on top.

In the cocktail biz, mini rounds of shots for the staff are often called "snaquiris," a little nip of something delish to keep spirits up. But also, if any cocktail were a snack, it'd be a Daiquiri.

VARIATIONS

Airmail: A Daiquiri meets a French 75. Shake up 1 ounce white rum, ½ ounce lime juice, ½ ounce honey syrup (page 163), then top with Prosecco.

Hemingway Daiquiri: Because Ernest himself was a diabetic, his Daiq was originally made without any sugar, but for a balanced cocktail, definitely add some. Use 2 ounces white rum, ¾ ounce lime juice, ½ ounce grapefruit juice, ½ ounce simple syrup, and ¼ ounce maraschino liqueur.

1½ ounces gin

¾ ounce lemon juice

¾ ounce simple syrup (page 162)

Seltzer, to top

1 orange slice and

   1 brandied cherry,

   or a lemon wedge,

   for garnish

Combine all the ingredients
except for the seltzer and
garnish in a shaker tin
with a few cubes of ice.

Shake until chilled, then
strain into an ice-filled
Collins glass and top
with seltzer. To lean into
tradition, garnish with an
orange slice and cherry on
a pick; otherwise, a lemon
wedge will do just fine.

TOM COLLINS

The Tom Collins is a timeless and satisfying mix of gin, lemon, and sugar, stretched long with some seltzer. (Long drinks, also called tall drinks, are cocktails served in a highball or Collins glass, often over ice.) Dating back to the late 1800s, the Tom Collins made such an impression on cocktail culture that it was given its own glass: the Collins glass.

You might roll your eyes when your grandpa orders one at dinner, but don't be so quick to scoff. A Tom Collins is light and refreshing, great for any time of day or night. It's also incredibly easy to make on a whim; you probably already have lemons and seltzer in your fridge. Whenever anyone suggests having a Tom Collins, I'm on board every time.

MARTINEZ

Considered the bridge between a Martini and a Manhattan, the Martinez is one of those forgotten classics that has regretfully remained forgotten. It's herbaceous, subtly fruity, and definitely booze-forward, with equal parts gin and sweet vermouth and a hint of maraschino liqueur.

If you can't decide between a Manhattan or a Martini, screw it—go with a Martinez! Be different! You'll certainly sound knowledgeable to your bartender and end up with a delicious drink to boot. If you're leaning toward a Manhattan vibe, go with a richer gin, like an Old Tom or genever. If you're feeling more Martini, stick with a London dry.

I've seen this cocktail made with Angostura bitters, orange bitters, or both. Olivia and I decided we liked orange bitters better, after some rigorous taste testing, of course. But if a Martinez is what twists your peel, experiment with the bitters and find what you like best.

VARIATION

Hanky Panky: One of the few old-school cocktails that can be traced back to a WOMAN! Ada Coleman invented this drink at the Savoy Hotel in London in the early twentieth century. It features that love-it-or-hate-it bittersweet liqueur Fernet-Branca. Just swap in the Fernet for the maraschino and omit the bitters.

1½ ounces gin
1½ ounces sweet vermouth
¼ ounce maraschino liqueur
3 dashes orange bitters
1 orange twist, for garnish

Combine all the ingredients except for the garnish in a mixing glass filled with ice. Stir until chilled, then strain into a Nick and Nora glass. Garnish with the orange twist and serve.

1 ounce gin OR Cognac

½ ounce lemon juice

½ ounce simple syrup
(page 162)

Prosecco, Champagne,
OR another dry
sparkling wine,
to top

1 lemon twist,
for garnish

Combine all the ingredients
except for the sparkling wine
and garnish in a shaker tin
with a few cubes of ice.

Shake until chilled, strain into a
flute OR coupe glass, and top with
sparkling wine. Garnish with
the lemon twist and serve.

French 75

When you want to be impressive but don't want to do a lot of heavy lifting, a French 75 will always answer your call. It's inherently a Tom Collins with sparkling wine instead of seltzer, and it looks oh-so elegant in a flute or a coupe glass. Whenever friends have someone special coming over for the first time and ask me what they should make, I tell them to go for a French 75. Tangy, fizzy, subtly sweet—it's a delightfully easy, elegant cocktail that's sure to nab you another date.

Gin is the common choice for a French 75 today, but there's also an iteration of the cocktail that uses Cognac as the base. Try 'em both and see which you like more. You get Champagne either way, and bubbles make everything better.

Gimlet

The Gimlet, which is essentially a Daiquiri with gin instead of rum, owes its creation to a nineteenth-century law that mandated the British merchant fleet stock rations of lime juice on board to prevent sailors from getting scurvy. The superior officers mixed gin into their lime to make it more palatable. So really, drinking a Gimlet is good for your health!

Besides being basically medicine, a Gimlet is super tasty. It's tart and delicate, a perfect foil to highlight whatever brand of gin you're using. You can also make your Gimlet with vodka instead of gin, if you'd like.

VARIATIONS

Southside: Add a handful of mint leaves to the tin and garnish with a fresh mint leaf on top.

Eastside: Muddle 3 cucumber slices, a handful of mint leaves, and the simple syrup in the bottom of your shaker tin, then add the gin and lime juice.

Gin Sour: Just replace the lime juice with lemon juice. You can even add an egg white, if you wanna!

Bee's Knees: Start with a Gin Sour but use honey syrup (page 163) instead of simple.

2 ounces gin
¾ ounce lime juice
¾ ounce simple syrup (page 162)
1 lime wheel, for garnish

Combine all the ingredients except for the garnish in a shaker tin filled with ice. Shake until chilled, then strain into a Nick and Nora or coupe glass. Garnish with the lime wheel and serve.

lime wheel
floating
on top

2 ounces bourbon

¾ ounce lemon juice

¾ ounce simple syrup (page 162)

1 lemon twist or lemon wedge,
   for garnish

Combine all the ingredients except for the garnish in a
shaker tin filled with ice. Shake until chilled,
then strain into a rocks glass over
fresh ice.

Garnish with the lemon twist
   or wedge and serve.

WHISKEY SOUR

There should be no surprises when you order this cocktail at a bar because the description is in the name! The Whiskey Sour is one of those drinks that was trendy for nearly a century, until the devil itself—artificial sour mix—took over cocktailing and absolutely ruined the Whiskey Sour's reputation. But a good version made with fresh citrus is stupid tasty, in both its non-egg-white and egg-white form.

VARIATIONS

Egg Sour: Add one large egg white to the tin and dry shake (page 170) then add ice and shake again until chilled. Double-strain into a coupe glass and garnish with dots of Angostura bitters on that pretty white canvas.

Gold Rush: Make it with honey syrup (page 163) instead of simple and serve on the rocks.

Penicillin: Use 2 ounces Scotch, ¾ ounce lemon juice, ½ ounce ginger syrup (page 162), and ¼ ounce honey syrup.

MARGARITA

The Margarita has the honor of being the most popular cocktail in America, but it's also celebrated the world over. Margarita is Spanish for "daisy," which is an old-school category of cocktail, defined as a sour with a little something extra (often an orange liqueur like triple sec).

When it's made well, a Margarita cocktail is a gorgeous symphony of agave spirit, fresh lime juice, and orange liqueur. Much like a Martini, it's also really variable: You can order it up or on the rocks, with a salt rim or no salt rim, with tequila or mezcal. Want it spicy? Want it fruity? Want it BOTH ways? Queen Marg can hang.

Blanco tequila is generally the move for a classic Margarita, but if you wanna be baller, go for the slightly aged, more expensive reposado tequila (make sure your other ingredients are just as top-notch, though). Also feel free to reduce the amount of triple sec and/or agave syrup in this recipe if it's a little too sweet for you. It'll always depend on how tart your limes are and the kind of triple sec you use, so adjust to your taste and ingredients.

Lime wedge
Kosher salt, to rim the glass (optional)
2 ounces tequila
¾ ounce lime juice
½ ounce triple sec
½ ounce agave syrup (page 163)

If desired, wet the side of a rocks or coupe glass with the lime wedge, then roll the rim in salt. Combine all the ingredients except for the lime wedge in a shaker tin filled with ice. Shake until chilled, then strain into a rocks glass over fresh ice or into a coupe glass.

Garnish with the lime wedge and serve.

1½ ounces tequila
¾ ounce grapefruit juice
½ ounce lime juice
½ ounce agave syrup
   (page 163)
Seltzer, to top
1 grapefruit twist,
   for garnish

Combine all the ingredients
except for the seltzer and
the garnish in a shaker tin
with a few cubes of ice.

Shake until chilled, then
strain into an ice-filled
Collins glass and top with
seltzer. Garnish with the
grapefruit twist and serve.

PALOMA

The Margarita tends to hog the spotlight as the go-to tequila classic, but don't sleep on Lady Paloma over here in the wings. She's juicy and fruity, insanely drinkable, and delightfully refreshing. Gimme a Paloma while I'm sitting on the edge of a pool with my feet in the water and my phone very far away.

Just as with the Margarita, using blanco tequila is typically the way to go. Traditionally, Palomas are made with Squirt grapefruit soda, but I like using fresh ingredients for optimal brightness.

VARIATION

Fancy Bartender-y Version: Instead of ½ ounce agave syrup, use ¼ ounce grapefruit liqueur and ¼ ounce agave syrup.

MOJITO

The Mojito is another drink that can be pretty contentious: folks argue whether it should be shaken or built in the glass, made with lime juice or muddled limes, and served over crushed or cubed ice. But most of us concur that it's white rum, lime, sugar, mint, and, more often than not, seltzer. It's a fun and lively combination that goes down real easy.

I'll never forget the time I was bartending on a slow Monday night and witnessed a proposal that erupted into an engagement party. (Super bold of those 30 folks to roll up to a bar without a reservation. I wouldn't recommend it, but hey, it worked out for them.) All I made the entire night were Mojitos, because that's what the couple drank on their first date. To me, a good Mojito is like a surprise engagement party in a glass.

Big handful of
    mint leaves
¾ ounce simple
    syrup (page 162)
1½ ounces white
    rum
¾ ounce lime
    juice
Seltzer, to top
1 mint bouquet,
    for garnish

Gently muddle the mint
leaves and simple syrup at
the bottom of a Collins
glass. Add the rum and lime
juice, then fill the glass
halfway with crushed ice.

Mix with a barspoon to
incorporate. Add
seltzer and more
crushed ice to
fill the glass.

Garnish with a mint bouquet and serve with a straw.

1 ounce Goslings Black Seal rum
1 ounce Smith & Cross Jamaican rum
¾ ounce lime juice
½ ounce almond orgeat
¼ ounce triple sec
1 mint bouquet, for garnish
1 orange half-moon, for garnish
Pineapple fronds,
   for garnish
   (optional)

Combine all the ingredients
except for the garnishes
in a shaker tin with a
bit of crushed ice.

Shake until you can no
longer hear the ice, then
pour into any fun glass you
want and fill with crushed ice.
Garnish with the mint bouquet and
orange half-moon and add, if you want,
pineapple fronds or a paper
umbrella—whatever!

Mai Tai

Maybe considered the king of tropical cocktails, a Mai Tai is refreshing, delightful, and often terribly made. ("Tropical" is the word the industry is now embracing for the cocktail genre once called "tiki.") It's usually just a random combination of rum, juice, and syrups: pineapple, coconut, flavored rums, grenadine. None of those have any business being in a Mai Tai. In essence, a Mai Tai is a Margarita with rum instead of tequila and orgeat instead of agave. Orgeat ("OR-jat") is a sugar syrup made with almonds that is commonly used in a lot of tropical drinks. A good Mai Tai is a harmonious balance of sour, sweet, nutty, funky, fruity—it's the whole package!

In my Mai Tai, I like using equal parts of a rich, full-bodied rum, like Goslings Black Seal, and a funky Jamaican rum, like Smith & Cross. But you can use the rums you have on hand, make your own blends, and have a good time. That's what tropical cocktails are all about.

CAIPIRINHA

A Caipirinha ("kai-per-EEN-ya") is a delicious, straightforward, three-ingredient drink of cachaça, lime, and sugar that transports you right to Brazil, even if you've never been there.

Cachaça, the headlining spirit in this cocktail, is distilled from fermented sugarcane juice. It has been made in Brazil for a long, long, long time and is produced all over the country. Cachaça can technically be called rum, because it's made from sugarcane, but it can ONLY be made in Brazil from fresh cane juice, so it's in a category all its own. It's grassy, it's sweet, it's fresh and a little fruity. It can be aged or unaged; most commonly an unaged cachaça (also called cachaça prata, meaning "silver") is used in a Caipirinha.

The Caipirinha is the drink that makes cachaça sing. It brings out its unique and complex characteristics, while still having the DNA of many drinks we know and love. The best part of a Caipirinha is its texture—because the shaken limes are dumped straight into the glass, you get all the chewy, pulpy goodness. For even more texture, you can use granulated sugar instead of simple syrup; however, I find that simple tends to mix better and makes for a more balanced cocktail.

½ lime, quartered
¾ ounce simple syrup (page 162)
2 ounces cachaça prata

Muddle the lime quarters and simple syrup in the bottom of your shaker tin, then add the cachaça and fill with ice. Shake until chilled, then pour the contents of the shaker into a rocks glass.

Add a couple more ice cubes, if needed, and serve.

1½ ounces vodka

¾ ounce lime juice

½ ounce ginger syrup (page 162)

Seltzer, to top

1 piece candied ginger, for garnish

1 lime wedge, for garnish

Combine all the ingredients except for the seltzer and garnishes in a shaker tin with a few cubes of ice. Shake until chilled, then strain into an ice-filled Collins glass or mule mug.

Top with seltzer, garnish with a piece of candied ginger and a lime wedge, and serve.

MOSCOW MULE

When the Moscow Mule first leapt onto the bar scene in the mid-twentieth century, it became one of the first popular vodka cocktails in the U.S. It's easy to understand why: the spice of the ginger pairs well with the citrusy lime, and the vodka provides a blank slate so the drink goes down smooth and easy. Put it all in an adorable copper mug, and it's no wonder that the Moscow Mule quickly emerged as a classic with staying power.

Although the original recipe calls for vodka, lime juice, and ginger beer, you don't have to stick to the Moscow Mule's roots. I enjoy using homemade ginger syrup and seltzer in lieu of ginger beer. Its namesake mule mug is traditional, but I say put it in whatever vessel you want, whether it's a rocks glass, Collins glass, mug, or julep cup. Use crushed ice or regular cubed ice, but, uh, definitely use ice of some sort.

VARIATIONS

Lazy Version: Just add vodka and lime juice directly to your glass of choice. Add ice, top with ginger beer, and stir.

Kentucky Mule: Use bourbon instead of vodka.

Gin Gin Mule: Use gin instead of vodka and add a handful of mint leaves to the shaker tin. Garnish with a mint bouquet.

Dark 'n Stormy: Just use dark rum instead of vodka! Goslings is the guy you want for the job.

SAZERAC

What a weird and wonderful drink. The Sazerac is a New Orleans cocktail gem and dates back to the late 1800s. Made of rye, sugar, and bitters, on paper it reads just like an Old Fashioned—but with some pretty distinct differences.

After the base of rye and a hint of sugar, the element that's essential to a classic Sazerac is Peychaud's bitters, a native New Orleans product. Peychaud's kind of tastes like anise and cherry, but it's hard to say what's in it for sure because the recipe is a closely guarded secret. A Sazerac's got some absinthe in there, too, usually just a rinse for that licorice-y aroma. It gets a lemon twist expressed over the top but not dropped in the glass. Finally it's served WITHOUT ICE but still in a ROCKS GLASS. Bizarre, I know, but congratulations, now you have a doctorate in Sazerac-making!

I've always stirred up my Sazeracs with just Peychaud's bitters, but one of my good bartender friends makes his with both Peychaud's and Angostura, and I gotta say it's awesome. So throw some Ango in there, too, if you're feeling feisty.

Absinthe, to rinse the glass
2 ounces rye
½ ounce demerara syrup (page 162)
5 dashes Peychaud's bitters
1 lemon twist

Rinse (page 172) a rocks glass with absinthe. Combine the rye, demerara syrup, and bitters in a mixing glass filled with ice. Stir until chilled, then strain into the prepared glass sans ice.

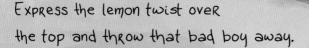

Express the lemon twist over the top and throw that bad boy away.

¾ ounce Rye
¾ ounce brandy
¾ ounce sweet vermouth
¼ ounce Bénédictine
2 dashes each Angostura and
  Peychaud's bitters
1 lemon twist, for garnish

Combine all the ingredients except for the garnish in a rocks glass over one big ice cube and stir until chilled. Garnish with the lemon twist and serve.

VIEUX CARRÉ

For a taste of a spirit-forward, vintage cocktail, look no further than this New Orleans classic, the Vieux Carré ("voo-kuh-RAY"), a 1930s original from the Carousel Bar at the Hotel Monteleone in the French Quarter. Less well known than its cousin Sir Sazerac, it's strong, rich, and herbaceous. The split base of rye, Cognac, and sweet vermouth really feels like the Three Musketeers of cocktailing: each plays its part, but no one's obnoxiously going for a solo. They get a helping hand from their friend Bénédictine, a French herbal liqueur that gives the cocktail a slightly floral, honeyed sweetness. A Vieux Carré is a great introduction to brandy for whiskey drinkers—or those who like both and don't want to choose!

While traditionally the brandy of choice is Cognac (the French connection and all), it's not a requirement; any aged grape brandy will do.

Mint Julep

Indisputably, the cocktail most connected with the American South is the Mint Julep. A flavorful combo of bourbon, mint, sugar, and crushed ice, it's a deliciously refreshing yet spirit-forward drink. It's probably one of the oldest cocktails around, since it was originally used medicinally (much like its peer, the Gimlet), but it became the drink of the Kentucky Derby in the 1930s. Technically, it's an Old Fashioned, just subbing in mint for the bitters. (This blew my mind so much that I actually had to walk it off.) But the best thing about this drink, in my humble opinion, is what it's served in: a julep cup! I always give bonus points to drinks that come with their own namesake glass ('sup, Tom Collins and Moscow Mule). I may never have been to Kentucky or the Derby, but every time I have a Mint Julep, I'm basically wearing an enormous hat and cheering on a horse I bet too much money on. It's a delight.

The key to a mouthwatering Mint Julep is plenty of fresh mint, lots of crunchy crushed ice, and bourbon. Unlike other whiskey cocktails, bourbon's a nonnegotiable here, lest you make a Southerner very, very mad.

VARIATION

Whiskey Smash: A Mint Julep meets a Whiskey Sour. Muddle 3 lemon wedges and a handful of mint with ¾ ounce simple syrup in a shaker tin. Add 1½ ounces whiskey, then fill with ice. Shake, then pour all of it into a rocks glass. Garnish with a mint bouquet and a fresh lemon wedge.

1 big ol' handful of mint leaves

¾ ounce simple syrup (page 162)

2 ounces bourbon

1 mint bouquet, for garnish

Muddle the mint leaves with the simple syrup in a 12-ounce serving glass, preferably a julep cup. Add the bourbon and fill the glass halfway with crushed ice.

Mix with a barspoon to incorporate. Add more crushed ice to fill. Garnish with the mint bouquet, and serve with a straw.

If desired, wet the side of a coupe glass with water
or a citrus wedge, then roll the rim in sugar. Combine
all the remaining ingredients except for the garnish in
a shaker tin filled with ice. Shake until chilled, then
strain into the coupe
glass, garnish
with the orange
twist, and
serve.

1 citrus wedge, to rim the
    glass (optional)
Granulated sugar, to rim the
    glass (optional)
2 ounces Cognac
¾ ounce lemon juice
¾ ounce triple sec
¼ ounce simple syrup (page 162)
1 orange twist, for garnish

SIDECAR

Many people are less familiar with brandy than with whiskey or gin, but the Sidecar is the ultimate gateway to brandy cocktails. It's essentially a Cognac Sour with orange liqueur, and it's downright delectable. It was reportedly invented by an American army captain in Paris in World War I who drove around in a motorcycle sidecar. I don't care if this story is true; I'm obsessed with the idea of a man in uniform drinking a Sidecar in a sidecar.

One time, I had a guy come to the bar and ask for a Hennessy and cranberry. He was dismayed when I told him we didn't have Hennessy OR cranberry juice. He said he just wanted something refreshing with Cognac, so I made him a Sidecar and he absolutely loved it! Those are my favorite moments behind the bar, introducing someone to their new go-to classic cocktail. I feel like a matchmaker.

I'm not entirely sure why, but after some serious, scientific taste testing, I've decided that Cognac is the best brandy to use in a Sidecar. The brand of triple sec you use will greatly affect the drink also (my personal fave to use in this cocktail is Pierre Ferrand dry curaçao). You don't have to rim the glass with sugar, but since Sidecars can lean on the drier side, I find it helps to balance the cocktail. Plus, who doesn't love a good sugar rim?

Boulevardier

A Boulevardier is a Negroni with bourbon instead of gin, purportedly created by an American in Paris during Prohibition and named after the magazine he edited. (Wow, those Americans really drank their way through Europe in the early twentieth century, didn't they?) But for all the simplicity of the gin-bourbon substitution, it's a lot more than just a Negroni variation. The Campari and sweet vermouth play off each other in a similar way, but while a Negroni is clean and lean, a Boulevardier is full-bodied and luxurious. Unlike the Negroni, it can be served on the rocks OR up, because the bourbon can hold its own in a way that gin can't. (Sorry, gin, no disrespect; please forgive me, I love you.) That being said, I much prefer it over a big rock that I can swirl around in the glass while I pontificate about the state of the world, as I imagine most American expat writers did in the 1920s.

VARIATIONS

Old Pal: Just use rye instead of bourbon and dry vermouth instead of sweet. Garnish with a lemon twist.

La Rosita: She's like a Boulevardier who got her motorcycle license against her parents' wishes and is now joyriding through the desert. Use 1½ ounces reposado tequila; ½ ounce each of sweet vermouth, dry vermouth, and Campari; and 1 dash Angostura bitters, then stir over a big ice cube and garnish with a lemon twist.

1½ ounces bourbon
¾ ounce sweet vermouth
¾ ounce Campari
1 orange twist, for garnish

One of Olivia's
faves, after years
of thinking that
she didn't like
"brown liquor"

Combine all the ingredients
except for the garnish in a
rocks glass over one big ice cube. Stir until chilled,
then garnish with the orange twist and serve.

2 ounces pisco
¾ ounce simple syrup (page 162)
½ ounce lime juice
½ ounce lemon juice
1 large egg white
Angostura bitters, for garnish

Just drag a cocktail
pick through the
Angostura dots to
make hearts

Combine all the ingredients
except for the garnish in a
shaker tin. Dry shake (page
170), then add ice and shake
again until chilled.

Double-strain into a coupe
glass, dot the bitters on top
of the drink to garnish, and
serve.

Pisco Sour

Pisco is an unaged, grape-based brandy from South America, most famous in the U.S. for its titular role in the Pisco Sour. (It would be beyond absurd if a Pisco Sour was made with, say, Scotch.) Pisco is the national spirit of both Chile and Peru, with both countries laying claim to being the spirit's birthplace. I'm gonna take the Swiss approach here and remain neutral. Both Peruvian and Chilean piscos are great, truly!

In this cocktail, pisco's intensely floral characteristics are mellowed out with citrus, sugar, and an egg white. Instead of just lemon OR lime, both are used, so the milder lemon balances out the more pungent lime. A Pisco Sour is a real joy: aromatic, frothy, sunny. It's the kind of sour that makes you salivate, and the only remedy is drinking more of it. If, when you think of brandy, only Cognac comes to mind, I dare you to try a Pisco Sour; it'll change your perception of what the spirit can be.

APEROL Spritz

Back in 2019, the *New York Times* published an article describing why an Aperol Spritz is not a good drink. It wasn't in the Opinion section, but rather in the Food section. Needless to say, it sparked an OUTRAGE to put it mildly. The comments even included someone calling the article "as inflammatory as the recipe for pea guacamole." Yikes!

I think the real issue is that people don't like being told what's good and what's bad. (Turns out the author of that article just doesn't like Aperol, and that's fine!) "Good" is subjective. If you like it, it's good. And A LOT of people like an Aperol Spritz, including me! The base of the cocktail is the classic Italian bitter aperitif Aperol, which is mixed with some sparkling wine (usually Prosecco) and seltzer. An Aperol Spritz is a perfect afternoon delight—it's sweet but not overly so, fizzy, refreshing, slightly bitter, a touch fruity. Plus it's served in a giant wine glass loaded with ice—you've gotta drink this during the day while wearing big glamorous sunglasses. *Salute!*

1½ ounces Aperol

2 ounces seltzer

Prosecco, to top

1 orange half-moon, for garnish

1 green olive on a cocktail pick,
for garnish (optional)

Combine the Aperol and the seltzer in a wine glass and fill with ice. Top with the Prosecco, then garnish with the orange half-moon and the olive, if you're feeling super Italian, and serve.

VARIATION

DIY Spritz: Aperol may be the most popular base for this cocktail, but you don't need it to make a spritz. In fact, you can make a spritz with nearly any liqueur, fortified wine, or amaro you have. St-Germain, Lillet, Montenegro—the possibilities are endless!

Combine all the ingredients except for the garnish in a shaker tin filled with ice. Shake until chilled, then strain into a coupe glass.

Garnish with the lime wheel and serve.

the infamous Martini glass, tall and precarious

2 ounces vodka

¾ ounce triple sec

½ ounce lime juice

½ ounce cranberry juice

¼ ounce simple syrup (page 162)

1 lime wheel, for garnish

COSMO

The pink drink to end all pink drinks. The Cosmopolitan survived the Cocktail Dark Ages of the 1990s and is now considered a true classic. This cocktail was already popular before *Sex and the City* catapulted it to celebrity-status—it's pink and has vodka, so why wouldn't it be? It's also part of the reason why giant Martini glasses were around for so long; it was super chic to drink a Cosmo from one of those sloshy 10-ounce vessels like Carrie and her crew did. Thankfully, the industry's simmered down a bit, and we can drink our Cosmos out of coupes without accidentally spilling on our Manolos.

A good Cosmo is tart and fruity, sweet but not saccharine, and let's admit it, a lot of fun. You can also use what you have around the house: citrus vodka or regular, natural unsweetened cranberry juice or Ocean Spray, any triple sec you stock in your bar. Do yourself a favor and use fresh lime juice, please.

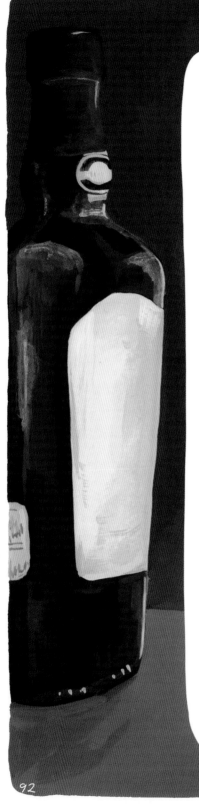

And now for something completely different: the Flip! It's quite possible you've never heard of this old-timey cocktail, because it's just a bizarre combo of liquor, sugar, and a whole egg. For real. It's decadent and cozy, like a hand-me-down cashmere sweater. Flips were traditionally made with fortified wine, such as sherry, or an aged higher-proof spirit like brandy or rum. Whatever you decide on, you want a base that's rich and flavorful, something that can hold its own next to an ENTIRE EGG, which, when emulsified, gets creamy and luscious. A Flip couldn't care less about your diet. Frankly, neither should you if you're gonna have one. It's a dessert cocktail; treat yo'self.

I prefer using ruby port in a Flip for some lovely fruitiness, but you can also go for a medium- or full-bodied sherry, Cognac, or your favorite aged rum.

FLIP

2 ounces ruby port
½ ounce demerara syrup (page 162)
1 large egg
Freshly grated nutmeg, for garnish

Combine all the
ingredients except for
the garnish in a shaker
tin. Dry shake (page 170),
then add ice and shake
again until chilled. Double-
strain into a coupe glass,
garnish with freshly grated
nutmeg, and serve.

1½ ounces gin

1 ounce raspberry syrup (page 164)

¾ ounce lemon juice

1 large egg white

1 raspberry skewered on a cocktail pick, for garnish

Combine all the ingredients except for the garnish in a shaker tin. Dry shake (page 170), then add ice and shake again until chilled.

dangerously drinkable

Double-strain into a coupe glass, garnish with the raspberry, and serve.

CLOVER CLUB

At the end of my first-ever training shift at Sweet Polly, the bar where I eventually became head bartender, I was asked to make my favorite classic cocktail. I spotted some raspberry syrup on the bar, so I made a Clover Club. And while I chose it mostly because I wanted to show off my fancy one-handed egg-cracking trick in the hopes of getting hired, this cocktail is definitely one of my all-time faves.

To me, a Clover Club is a perfectly balanced Gin Sour. It's tart from the lemon juice, juicy from the raspberries, and silky smooth from the fluffy cloud of egg white. The botanicals in the gin play with these elements so well, and all four ingredients blend together like a barbershop quartet, minus the straw hats.

It just so happens that Clover Club is also one of my favorite bars in Brooklyn, and Olivia and I have enjoyed many, many of their eponymous cocktails. For a long time I thought the bar preceded the drink, but it's the other way around. They still make the best one I've ever had, though.

PIÑA COLADA

When you think of a Piña Colada, you might automatically envision drinking one at a poolside bar on a tropical beach resort. And yeah, that sounds beyond delightful. But you can make a Piña Colada yourself, without a slushy machine or any artificial syrups, in the comfort of your own home. All it takes is some rum, fresh pineapple juice, and coconut cream. Some folks in the biz say that a Piña Colada is a Flip variation, since it fills the bill of booze, sugar, and something creamy and fatty. I asked my go-to source for all things tropical drinks, my friend and Sweet Polly coworker Tom, what he thought of this. He said, "If a Piña Colada is a Flip, then Avril Lavigne is punk." Bartenders are very opinionated people.

I like to use a base of light rum with a touch of a deeper, richer rum for an additional depth of flavor in my Piña Coladas. And instead of throwing it all in a blender, I prefer this cocktail shaken and served over crushed ice. It's just as refreshing without venturing into milkshake territory.

You can buy coconut cream at most grocery stores (Coco Lopez is my trusted brand), but you can also make your own by combining equal parts full-fat coconut milk and simple syrup. Add a few pinches of salt, whisk away, and you're good to go.

2 ounces white rum
½ ounce blackstrap rum
1½ ounces pineapple juice
1½ ounces coconut
    cream
1 pineapple wedge,
    for garnish
1 brandied cherry,
    for garnish

Combine all the ingredients
except for the garnishes in
a shaker tin with a bit of
crushed ice. Shake until you
can no longer hear the ice,
then pour the entire contents of
the shaker into a rocks glass (or
whatever fun glass you want). Fill with
additional crushed ice, garnish with the
pineapple wedge, the cherry, and a
paper umbrella (if you're feeling
especially beachy), and serve.

2 ounces gin

¾ ounce lemon juice

¼ ounce maraschino liqueur

¼ ounce crème de violette

¼ ounce simple syrup (page 162)

1 brandied cherry on a cocktail pick,
   for garnish

Combine all the
ingredients except
for the garnish in a shaker
tin filled with ice. Shake until
chilled, then strain into a Nick
and Nora or a coupe glass.

Garnish with the cherry and serve.

AVIATION

In 2015, when I was just setting out on my bartending journey, I went on a date with a guy who worked for a gin brand. Before I could even utter a single word to the bartender, he ordered me an Aviation. People ordering for me is one of my biggest pet peeves (I can speak for myself, thank you very much), so I did not have high hopes. Well, I certainly made a love connection that night—needless to say, it was NOT with the gin rep. He didn't get a second date, but I've been having a romantic affair with gin and Aviations ever since.

The Aviation cocktail dates back to the early twentieth century. It's floral, delicate, and all about balance. The maraschino liqueur brings an elegant cherry sweetness, and the citrusy lemon juice keeps it crisp. But an Aviation is not an Aviation without crème de violette, a violet-flower liqueur that's aromatic and botanical. Be careful not to use too much; it can become soapy real fast.

OAXACA Old·Fashioned

A modern classic is a drink that was invented after the cocktail revival of the early 2000s and is now so well-known that bartenders are expected to know how to make it, just like they do a Daiquiri. There's no question that one of the most famous modern classics is the Oaxaca Old Fashioned, created back in 2007 by bartender Phil Ward at the renowned cocktail bar Death & Co in New York City. This was right as tequila was beginning its climb up the popularity ladder and mezcal was still relatively obscure in the United States. It has the same structure as a classic Old Fashioned but showcases the savory and smoky qualities of tequila and mezcal, respectively. At that time, taking agave spirits in a stirred direction was pretty rare, so this drink is a game-changer that showed a lot of folks you can do more with them than just make a Margarita.

Now, flaming an orange twist may sound like a euphemism for something that happens in Vegas and should stay there. Really, you're just gently heating the twist with a match and expressing its oils over the flame. It deepens the flavor of the oils by lightly caramelizing them, which is perfect for this cocktail. It doesn't hurt that it's one very cool pyro party trick, too.

*To flame the orange twist, light a match, then hold the twist by its sides over the glass, skin side facing down. Place the lit match between the glass and the twist, squeeze the twist sharply over the match, and watch the citrus oils go up in flame. Make sure to hold the twist far enough above the glass so smoke residue doesn't get in your drink.

1½ ounces reposado tequila

½ ounce mezcal

Barspoon of agave syrup (page 163)

2 dashes Angostura bitters

1 orange twist, for garnish

Combine all the ingredients except for the garnish in a mixing glass filled with ice. Stir until chilled, then strain into a rocks glass over one big ice cube. Garnish with the orange twist, either flamed* or not, and serve.

¾ ounce gin

¾ ounce lime juice

¾ ounce green Chartreuse

¾ ounce maraschino liqueur

Combine all the ingredients in a shaker tin filled with ice.

Shake until chilled, then strain into a Nick and Nora or coupe glass. No garnish!

Last Word

An equal-parts drink for the ages, the Last Word is a Prohibition-era cocktail with gin, lime juice, green Chartreuse, and maraschino liqueur in, well, equal parts. It's refreshing yet has a strong bite to it. The aromatic maraschino softens out the herbaceous Chartreuse, the lime keeps it mouthwatering, and the gin is like the juniper glue that holds it all together. If you wanna switch it up and get some smoke in the mix, swap in mezcal for the gin. Or use aquavit instead for some additional savoriness. Plenty of fun twists on this classic.

As for the garnish, I firmly believe a cherry does NOT belong, whether it's dropped in the glass or skewered on a pick. I've gotten into many, many obnoxiously long and pointless debates about this. The cocktail is perfect on its own and IT DOESN'T NEED A CHERRY. The defense rests.

Shockingly, I've never heard anyone fight about the recipe. Looks like the Last Word did really have the last word on that, at least.

Original
Cocktails

Creating Originals

Congratulations! You've learned the fundamentals of drinkmaking and sipped your way through many classics of the cocktail canon. Now that you've aced Cocktailing 101, it's time to break the mold—kind of like how in acting school you have to study Shakespeare before you can make weird, modernist dance theater.

I think about creating cocktails in the same way that I think about cooking. When you first start learning how to cook, you don't just go in blindly without any guidance; otherwise you'd burn your parents' house to the ground. You begin by using recipes and stick with recipes for a while. Once you become comfortable, that's when you start experimenting. You look in your pantry and think about what you could do with what you have or what ingredients to buy for something new you want to make. Sometimes you riff on a classic dish. Sometimes you make something you've never tasted before. Sometimes you realize you don't have an ingredient at the last minute and have to improvise. A lot of times you fail and are like "Oh, I'm never making this again." But other times you succeed and have a new signature dish that you can make for yourself and share with others. Creating cocktails is no different.

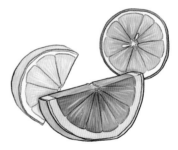

There are many ways to go about inventing original cocktails. Here are the two main strategies I like to use and how I apply them.

STRATEGY 1: MR. POTATO HEAD® THEORY

I cannot take credit for this brilliant yet simple approach to cocktail invention. Acclaimed New York City bartender Phil Ward came up with this one when he worked at Death & Co. The idea is to take a classic cocktail formula and sub in one element for another, like swapping out pieces on a Mr. Potato Head®. We've already seen countless examples of this scattered throughout the classic recipes. (Make a Negroni with bourbon instead of gin, and it's now a Boulevardier.) It's easiest to start with switching up the base spirit in a classic recipe, then you can start substituting other elements, like juices, sweeteners, and liqueurs. Not every change will be a one-to-one substitution, and you'll probably have to adjust the ratios in order to get a balanced drink. When you've reached a delicious final result, Mr. Potato Head® might have eyes for a nose and lips for an ear, but you've done it! A brand-new cocktail that has its origins in a tried-and-true classic.

STRATEGY 2: RATATOUILLE METHOD

Yes, both of my cocktail-creating strategies reference Pixar movies.

But I get a lot of inspiration from a scene in *Ratatouille* where Remy, a budding young rat chef, is explaining flavor pairings to his rodent brother. He has a grape in one paw and a piece of cheese in another; each on its own has a distinct flavor, but put them together and you get an entirely new taste. This absolutely works for cocktails when you think about the core flavors of different ingredients. For the Papa Don't Peach (page 127), I paired spicy rye with fruity apple brandy, since spice and fruit balance each other out. Apples and honey are one of my favorite flavor combos, so honey syrup seemed like a good sweetener to use. Cinnamon loves these ingredients, too, and would give the cocktail a hint of baking spice.

The final element was inviting peach liqueur to the party, who already has these dudes on speed dial. The combination of all these different tastes results in a harmonious drink that has a new flavor all its own.

So we've got these two ways of creating original cocktails. Now it's time to implement them. (This may or may not have been influenced by the classic Bop It!® toy of my childhood.)

Step 1: Dream it!

This is the concept for your drink. It could be a Negroni variation. It could be the flavor of kiwi. It could also be more abstract, like a great cocktail name (i.e., Threat Level Midnight, page 149, in honor of *The Office*) or a mood ("cozy yet destructive" inspired the All-Nighter on page 157). One time the concept for a drink was pulled straight from my subconscious (see the cocktail of my literal dreams, the Velour Tracksuit on page 130).

Step 2: Plan it!

Before you even pick up a bottle, decide what the focus of the cocktail will be. If you're making a Negroni variation, take the Negroni formula and decide what you want to alter. If you're interested in a particular key ingredient, like Chartreuse or kiwi, consider what will go well with that flavor. Have a blueprint in mind before you spend your whole paycheck on cocktail experimentation.

CHARTREUSE

Step 3: Try it!

This step is about nailing down your ingredients. Test out your first sample recipe. You might be able to identify what works and what doesn't. Trust your palate! Then try it again another way, maybe with a split base of two liquors, or with a different flavored syrup, or with some bitters this time. Rarely will you get it right on your first attempt. Sometimes you discover that what you originally had in mind was a TERRIBLE idea, and you have to start over (I will never live down the horror of my radish-mezcal venture).

Step 4: Tweak it!

Once you have your ingredients set, keep making different versions, adjusting only one thing at a time. Is it too acidic? Try it with less citrus. Is it now too sweet? Bump up the liquor. It's gonna feel tedious, but patience is a virtue, tipsy grasshopper. Then start considering things like glassware and garnish, keeping in mind that they should enhance the deliciousness of the drink.

Step 4½: Share it!

Get other palates involved. I consider this a half step because I guess it's not required. But cocktails are more fun when they're shared! Plus someone has to drink all those rejects, right?

Once you settle on your final recipe, for the love of God, WRITE IT DOWN. Then relax and go drink your completely original cocktail! You've earned it.

Blonde Ambition

Tom Collins's hot cousin

This is one of the first cocktails I ever invented, and it has become my signature. It's in the Tom Collins (page 55) family, having the elements of liquor, sweet, sour, and bubbles, served long over ice. Gin loves hanging out with fresh produce, so raspberry and cucumber keep things fresh and bright. Yellow Chartreuse, a slightly sweet French liqueur, provides herbaceousness, and Amaro Montenegro adds a slight bitter edge. Finally, the Blonde Ambition is topped off with Prosecco for a fizzy kick. It's easy to drink yet still packs a punch. When I was initially creating it, I was told by several people (who hadn't tried it yet) that it had too many ingredients that wouldn't work together, but they were wrong. It's an ambitious drink, and I'm an ambitious blonde.

3 cucumber slices, plus 1 for garnish
1½ ounces gin
¾ ounce lime juice
½ ounce yellow Chartreuse
½ ounce raspberry
    syrup (page 164)
¼ ounce Amaro
    Montenegro
Prosecco, to top
1 raspberry skewered
    on a cocktail
    pick, for garnish

Muddle 3 of the cucumber slices in the bottom of a shaker tin, then add the remaining ingredients except for the Prosecco and the garnishes.

Add a few cubes of ice and shake until chilled, then double-strain into an ice-filled Collins glass. Top with Prosecco, garnish with the remaining cucumber slice and the raspberry, and serve.

1½ ounces bourbon

¾ ounce blanc vermouth

¾ ounce strawberry-infused
   Campari (page 165)

1 strawberry slice, for garnish

Combine all the ingredients except for the garnish in a rocks glass over one big ice cube. Stir until chilled, garnish with the strawberry slice, and serve.

ABBEY ROAD

I was interested in making a classic Boulevardier (page 84) feel lighter for warmer weather, since I like drinking bourbon in every season. Strawberry-infused Campari brings a subtle fruitiness to the cocktail, and the strawberries go beautifully with Campari's orange notes. Blanc vermouth keeps it delicate and lets the strawberry flavor shine, but it's definitely still a spirit-forward cocktail, thanks to our ol' pal bourbon.

If you're hesitant about making a specialty ingredient, just know that this strawberry Campari is good in basically EVERYTHING. It also makes classic bitter cocktails more approachable.

Woman of Destiny

There was one afternoon at Sweet Polly when a case of crème de violette, a violet-flower-flavored liqueur, accidentally got delivered instead of the product that we actually needed. My old manager handed me a bottle and said, "Do something with this, please." So I did. I never say no to a challenge.

Violette isn't known for much except Aviations (page 99), so that was a natural starting point. Smoky mezcal seemed like an unconventional element to pair with flowers, but I was curious how they would go together. Splendidly, it turns out! Grapefruit works super well with smoky flavors but also rocks out with more floral ingredients, so it provides a perfect bridge between these two seemingly disparate elements. When thinking about a sweetener, aromatic honey came to mind, rounding out the cocktail and giving it more body. And there she was! The Woman of Destiny was born.

1¾ ounces mezcal
½ ounce lemon juice
½ ounce grapefruit juice
½ ounce honey syrup (page 163)
¼ ounce crème de violette
1 edible flower or grapefruit twist,
    for garnish

Combine all the
ingredients except for
the garnish in a shaker
tin filled with ice.
Shake until chilled, then
strain into a coupe glass.

Garnish with the edible
flower or grapefruit
twist and serve.

1½ ounces bourbon
½ ounce lemon juice
½ ounce St-Germain
½ ounce simple syrup (page 162)
1 dash Angostura bitters
Prosecco, to top
1 lemon twist, for garnish

Combine all the
ingredients except
for the Prosecco and
the garnish in a shaker tin
filled with ice. Shake until chilled,
then strain into a coupe glass.

Top with Prosecco, garnish with
the lemon twist, and serve.

St. Julie

Okay, this was ACTUALLY the first cocktail I ever invented, back when I was a green bartender working at a terrible restaurant on the Lower East Side and had no idea what I was doing. I pretty much threw all my favorite things in a tin and tasted what happened. Turns out, shaking whiskey, St-Germain elderflower liqueur, and Prosecco together wasn't gonna cut it. (As I now know, you shouldn't shake bubbles. You will destroy your outfit and your dignity.)

What I was missing was acid. Duh. Lemon juice and Angostura bitters needed to enter the chat. The result is a delicate yet complex whiskey version of a French 75 (page 59).

SAVE ROOM

One night when I was really craving an Old Fashioned (page 45) but was too lazy to make simple syrup (!), I looked in my fridge and was like "Ooh MAPLE syrup!" You can just make an Old Fashioned using Vermont's finest, but to take it up a notch, incorporate my other favorite thing to pair with maple: pecans! I don't know about you, but a maple-bourbon pecan pie is exactly what I want at the end of Thanksgiving dinner. So why not transform it into a luscious dessert cocktail you can enjoy at the end of ANY meal?

If you're like I was that fateful evening and the idea of making anything is too much, whatever whiskey you have on hand will still taste great. But this pecan bourbon is truly something special, whether it's for a specific occasion or just a regular Thursday night.

2 ounces Pecan-Infused Bourbon (page 166)
¼ ounce maple syrup
3 dashes orange bitters
1 orange twist, for garnish
Freshly grated nutmeg, for garnish

Combine all the ingredients except for the garnishes in a rocks glass over one big ice cube. Stir until chilled, then garnish with the orange twist and grated nutmeg and serve.

1 ounce Lillet Blanc
¾ ounce gin
¾ ounce Suze
½ ounce lemon juice
¼ ounce lime juice
1 large egg white
Orange bitters, for garnish

Combine all the ingredients except for the garnish in a shaker tin. Dry shake (page 170), then add ice and shake again until chilled.

Double-strain into a coupe glass, dot the surface of the drink with the orange bitters, and serve.

Robe Dorée

I love a good White Negroni (page 51) and wanted to make a refreshing shaken version. You know, for the times when you need to take a breather from the more spirit-forward sippers but still want something complex and biting. The floral, orangey Lillet highlights the earthy and fragrant notes in Suze, a dry, bitter French apéritif. Junipery gin rounds out that throuple nicely. At first, I just used lemon juice as the citrus, but it wasn't enough to cut through those three strong personalities. Taking a page out of Pisco Sour's (page 87) book, I added both lemon and lime juices; incorporating just a hint of lime adds a brightness not achieved by lemon alone. It's all tied together with an egg white, making it soft and silky. A few dots of orange bitters on top really bring out the aromatics, creating one dynamic, layered cocktail.

Verano Verde

To me, a classic Margarita (page 64) is ideal on a sweltering summer's day. So I added both St-Germain and cilantro to the base formula, two ingredients that to me scream, "Hello, I'm a garden!" to really lean into the summery vibe. Grapefruit juice imparts a little natural bitterness to balance out the sweetness of the elderflower, and the acidity of the lime makes sure it's still got the essence of a Marg.

If you're one of those people who was cursed with a tongue that thinks cilantro tastes like soap, I am so sorry for your loss. But there's still hope, because you can just as easily make this cocktail with basil instead.

Gently muddle the cilantro leaves and simple syrup in the bottom of a shaker tin. Add the remaining ingredients, except for the garnish, and fill with ice. Shake until chilled, then double-strain into a rocks glass over fresh ice. Garnish with the cilantro sprig and serve.

Handful of cilantro leaves

¼ ounce simple syrup (page 162)

2 ounces blanco tequila

¾ ounce grapefruit juice

½ ounce lime juice

½ ounce St-Germain

1 cilantro sprig, for garnish

MAD HATTER

The origin of this cocktail came during the week Olivia and I spent in Long Island way back in 2018, when we were first beginning to conceptualize this book. I wanted to make an evening version of the mug of Earl Grey tea Olivia enjoyed every morning. Vodka's neutrality is ideal for a tea infusion, and honey and lemon are tea's natural playmates. Earl Grey's strong bergamot flavor was tricky to balance, and I've gotta admit, balance eluded me for a while. (Okay, THREE YEARS.) Until I decided to double-down on the floral notes by adding St-Germain and crème de violette. Flowers on flowers on flowers, baby! It shouldn't work, but somehow it does. It's just kooky enough for Wonderland's famous tea drinker. (And for Olivia, of course.)

2 ounces Earl Grey-Infused Vodka
   (page 165)
½ ounce lemon juice
½ ounce St-Germain
¼ ounce crème de violette
¼ ounce honey syrup (page 163)
1 lemon wedge, for garnish

Combine all the ingredients except for the garnish in a shaker tin filled with ice. Shake until chilled, then strain into a teacup or mug over an ice sphere. Serve with the lemon wedge on a cute li'l saucer on the side.

Earl Grey Vodka
made ⁴/₇

1¼ ounces rye
¾ ounce apple brandy
⅓ ounce peach liqueur
¼ ounce honey syrup (page 163)
Barspoon of cinnamon syrup (page 163)
Freshly grated nutmeg, for garnish
1 peach slice, for garnish

this stuff slaps

Combine all the ingredients except for the garnishes in a mixing glass filled with ice.

Stir until chilled, then strain into a rocks glass over fresh ice. Grate fresh nutmeg on top, garnish with the peach slice, and serve.

PAPA · DON'T - PEACH -

Based on an Old Fashioned (page 45), this drink combines the best of fall and spring. I love putting rye and apple brandy together— the fruitiness of the apple really balances the spiciness of the rye. The peach liqueur amps up the bright qualities without making it too sweet. To lean into the fall characteristics of the cocktail, I added honey and just a touch of cinnamon. The result is strong yet approachable, ideal both for lounging in front of a fire in a cozy sweater AND for sitting on a porch swing admiring your blossoming garden.

for snacking

1½ ounces blanco tequila

¾ ounce kiwi honey (page 164)

½ ounce lime juice

¼ ounce strawberry liqueur

Seltzer, to top

1 kiwi wheel, for garnish

Combine all the ingredients except for the seltzer and the garnish in a shaker tin with a few cubes of ice. Shake until chilled, then strain into an ice-filled Collins glass. Top with seltzer, garnish with the kiwi wheel, and serve.

Gold Coast

Whenever it's time to R&D some new drinks, I go out to a bunch of bars and drink a lot of cocktails. You know, for research. At Bar Goto Niban, one of my local Brooklyn spots, they had a beautiful drink with gin and kiwi. It made me think about how I didn't see kiwi used in cocktails all that much. Tequila loves tropical flavors, and kiwi and strawberries are a match made in fruit-bowl heaven. In the spirit of a refreshing Paloma (page 67), I top it all off with seltzer to make it even more crushable.

The kiwi honey is essential to this cocktail, but if you don't have (or feel like buying) strawberry liqueur, just muddle some fresh strawberries in there. Or use the Strawberry Campari (page 165) you have on hand from making an Abbey Road (page 113)!

Velour Tracksuit

I know I'm gonna sound ridiculously woo-woo, but I promise it's true: this cocktail came to me in my dreams. I actually woke up in the middle of the night and thought, "A purple cocktail with velvet falernum called Velour Tracksuit." I was determined to make it happen.

Velvet falernum is fun to say and also fun to drink. It's a spiced Caribbean liqueur often used in tropical-style drinks, so I figured rum was a natural partner for it. Then I looked at the bottles at Sweet Polly for something purple. Crème de cassis immediately jumped out, because the black currant would pair excellently with ruby port, another purple ingredient! Adding a whole egg gives the cocktail the silky-smooth texture of a Flip (page 93), à la a classic velour tracksuit.

After a month of trial and error (and consuming at least three dozen raw eggs—I'm basically Rocky), the cocktail of my actual dreams was born.

1 ounce white rum

1 ounce ruby port

¾ ounce crème de cassis

½ ounce velvet falernum

3 dashes Angostura bitters

1 large egg

Freshly grated nutmeg, for garnish

Combine all the ingredients except for the garnish in a shaker tin. Dry shake (page 170), then add ice and shake again until chilled.

Double-strain into a coupe glass, garnish with the nutmeg, and serve.

Rosemary Tincture (page 165),
  to rinse the glass
2 ounces whiskey
1 ounce sweet vermouth
5 dashes Angostura bitters
1 fresh rosemary sprig, for garnish

Rinse (page 172) a Nick and Nora with the rosemary tincture. Combine all the ingredients except for the garnish in a mixing glass filled with ice. Stir until chilled, then strain into the prepared glass.

Garnish with the fresh rosemary sprig and serve.

Rosemary MANHATTAN

Okay, this is just a Manhattan (page 49) with rosemary. Sometimes it's as easy as that.

Rosemary is one of my favorite herbs, and its earthiness is a great counterpoint to the sweetness of the vermouth. A tincture is a way of adding a strong flavor into a cocktail by using drops, dashes, or rinses. It's an infusion that you shouldn't drink on its own because it would be way too intense— but here it enhances the aroma and flavor of the drink while still maintaining the essence of a classic Manhattan.

FORTUNE'S FOOL

I love a traditional Bramble, which is pretty much a Gin Sour (page 60) with blackberries. Ginger is also one of my favorite ingredients, and it pairs well with both gin AND blackberries, so I thought, "Why not make a ginger Bramble?" I'm very proud to say this was one of Sweet Polly's best-selling cocktails ever. One time a guy sat at the bar and drank FIVE of them while on the phone with his car insurance company!

The name is twofold: a fool is a traditional blackberry dessert, and the phrase "fortune's fool" comes from *Romeo and Juliet*, when Romeo kills his girlfriend's cousin. But you don't have to commit murder and get banished from Verona (or argue with Geico about your coverage) to enjoy this cocktail.

1½ ounces gin

½ ounce lemon juice

½ ounce ginger syrup (page 162)

½ ounce crème de mûre

3 dashes orange bitters

1 blackberry skewered on a cocktail
   pick, for garnish

Combine all the ingredients except for the garnish
in a shaker tin filled with ice

Shake until chilled, then strain into
a rocks glass over one big ice cube.
Garnish with the blackberry and serve.

1½ ounces Coconut-Washed Baijiu
    (page 166)
¾ ounce lime juice
¾ ounce simple syrup (page 162)
½ ounce white rum
1 edible flower or lime wheel,
    for garnish

Combine all
the ingredients
except for the garnish in
a shaker tin filled with ice.

Shake until chilled, then
double-strain into a
coupe glass.

Garnish with the edible flower
    or the lime wheel and serve.

Celestial Stem

This drink was a collab with my fellow Sweet Polly bartender Tom Wolfson. Baijiu ("BYE-gio") is a Chinese grain spirit that is by far the world's most popular liquor. (More baijiu is produced every year than both whiskey and vodka combined!) At the bar, I used Ming River brand, which is a light aroma Sichuan-style baijiu that has a floral, fruity, funky vibe happening. Honestly, I think this particular bottling tastes like a sour apple Jolly Rancher, which is a good thing, if you ask me.

Because the flavor of baijiu is pretty unfamiliar to a lot of Western palates, Tom and I wanted to take the drink in a direction beloved by cocktailers the world over: the Daiquiri (page 52). We decided to fat-wash the baijiu in coconut oil to soften its intense flavor. Fat-washing is a technique that adds savory flavors to spirits. Combine alcohol with a fatty ingredient, freeze it, skim off the solids, and you've got the flavor of the fat directly into the spirit. Sounds gross; tastes amazing.

DOCTOR'S ORDERS

I'll be honest, I'm not the biggest fan of Scotch. The peatiness often overwhelms me, and I've found that many Scotch cocktails aren't very balanced. So I wanted to make a Scotch cocktail for people like me, who maybe aren't as keen on the spirit Scots guzzle by the gallon.

Taking the best-known modern Scotch cocktail, the Penicillin (page 63), as a jumping-off point, I lightened up the smoky notes with a whole bunch of fruit. Raspberry is a terrifically bright flavor that holds its own against ginger. Because whiskey can get down with stone fruits, apricot comes in and shakes up the party. Smoky, sweet, spicy, sour: just what the doctor ordered!

2 ounces blended Scotch

¾ ounce lemon juice

½ ounce ginger syrup (page 162)

¼ ounce raspberry syrup (page 164)

¼ ounce apricot liqueur

1 raspberry and 1 piece candied
    ginger skewered on a cocktail
    pick, for garnish

Combine all the
ingredients except for
the garnish in a shaker tin filled
with ice. Shake until chilled, then strain into a rocks
glass over fresh ice. Garnish with the raspberry
and candied ginger and serve.

1 ounce rye

1 ounce apple brandy

¾ ounce sweet vermouth

¼ ounce Amaro Montenegro

1 dash Angostura bitters

1 orange twist snaked on a cocktail
pick, for garnish

Combine all the
ingredients except for
the garnish in a mixing
glass filled with ice.
Stir until chilled, then
strain into a Nick and
Nora glass. Garnish with
the orange twist and serve.

KING'S CO
BOURBON W
45% alcoho

Storm King

Olivia and I went to college in New York's Hudson Valley, prime apple country. I was interested in making a fall Manhattan (page 49) variation using American apple brandy, so I split the base with rye to balance the fruitiness, which resulted in something reminiscent of a spiced apple pie. A touch of Amaro Montenegro brings a light bittersweet note. It felt right to name this cocktail after Storm King Art Center, the sculpture garden in Beacon, New York, which is absolutely gorg in the fall. And the fun squiggle of the orange twist is an homage to the Andy Goldsworthy wall that lives there.

RY

ne. 200 ml

Honeycrisp

As a kid, I loved eating apples with honey. I would bite open honey sticks and smear them all over tart apple slices, making a sticky, juicy mess. Now that I am an adult of legal drinking age, I can transform one of my favorite childhood snacks into a cocktail!

Calvados, the apple brandy made in Normandy, has a sharp, funky flavor that goes beautifully with honey and tames its sweetness. Apples and honey are often eaten together on the Jewish holiday of Rosh Hashanah as a symbol of a sweet New Year. And everyone knows drinking bubbly for New Year's is effectively a requirement, so adding Prosecco turns this into a festive, low-ABV French 75 (page 59) riff.

1 ounce Calvados
¼ ounce honey syrup (page 163)
Prosecco or
    another
    dry
    sparkling
    wine, to top
1 grapefruit twist,
    for garnish

Combine the Calvados and
honey syrup in a coupe glass
or flute. Top with Prosecco
and stir gently with a barspoon.
Garnish with the grapefruit twist
and serve.

Rosemary tincture (page 165),
    to rinse the glass
1½ ounces rye
½ ounce lemon juice
½ ounce apricot liqueur
½ ounce honey syrup (page 163)
1 large egg white
1 fresh rosemary sprig,
    for garnish

Rinse (page 172) a coupe glass with the rosemary tincture. Combine the remaining ingredients, except for the garnish, in a shaker tin. Dry shake (page 170), then add ice and shake until chilled.

Double-strain into the prepared glass, garnish with the rosemary sprig, and serve.

Bobby McGee

Ever since I was 16, I've been in love with Janis Joplin. Her cover of "Me and Bobby McGee" is one of my favorite songs of all time. I don't know why, but something about the savory combination of rye, apricots, and rosemary makes me feel like I'm hitchhiking right alongside Janis and Bobby from Baton Rouge to New Orleans. Apricots and honey are a sublime pair. The egg white gives the cocktail a bit more body and takes it in a Whiskey Sour (page 63) direction. I think Janis (known lover of Southern Comfort, a fruit-flavored liqueur made from whiskey) would have appreciated this one.

← rosemary tincture in a spritz bottle

145

MEDIANOCHE

I cannot tell you how many times I've been asked for "something spicy with tequila" when I've been behind the bar. It's an understandable request: agave spirits and hot peppers are BFFs. Infusing tequila with jalapeños is a quick and easy way to get that fresh spice action. But instead of just making a regular ol' Margarita (page 64) with some jalapeños, I wanted to balance out the heat with a strong fruit flavor. Enter crème de mûre, which provides a rich blackberry counterpoint that goes so well with jalapeños and tequila. This is a punchy, refreshing, addictive cocktail that'll make you sweat a bit.

not for snacking

2 ounces Jalapeño-Infused Tequila
   (page 166)
¾ ounce simple syrup (page 162)
½ ounce lime juice
½ ounce crème de mûre
Seltzer, to top
1 lime wedge, for
   garnish

Combine all the
ingredients except for
the seltzer and garnish
in a shaker tin with
a few cubes of ice.
Shake until chilled, then
strain into an ice-filled
Collins glass.

Top with
seltzer, garnish
with the lime wedge,
and serve.

1½ ounces mezcal
½ ounce Cynar
½ ounce reposado tequila
½ ounce Nixta elote liqueur
1 lemon twist, for garnish

Combine all the
ingredients except for the
garnish in a rocks glass over one big ice cube.
Stir until chilled, then garnish with the lemon twist and serve.

Threat Level Midnight

I wanted to invent a mezcal-based sipper that was complex in flavor yet immensely drinkable. In a Oaxaca Old Fashioned (page 100), there's more reposado tequila than mezcal, but flipping that ratio lets the smokiness of the mezcal really shine. Cynar is a savory Italian amaro that gives this drink some bitterness, and Nixta, a Mexican elote liqueur that tastes like a freshly made corn tortilla, contributes an utterly unique sweetness. Nixta might be a little tricky to find, but if you do, grab a bottle or five off those shelves. You won't regret it.

As I know a lot of other people have done, I've watched all of *The Office* many, many times. So this one's an homage to Michael Scott's homemade crime-action movie, "Threat Level Midnight." It's a little dangerous, a crowd-pleaser, and down for repeat consumption.

Cynar helps balance out the smoke

GEOGRAPHY MINOR

Fun fact about me: I was a drama major in college, but I also minored in geography. (Liberal arts colleges, am I right?) In honor of this weird bit of trivia about my life, I decided to make a nonalcoholic riff on an Eastside (page 60), because now my great sense of direction is all my minor is really good for. (Also, minors can partake. Get it?)

Cucumber, mint, citrus—I'm not reinventing the wheel here. Since I'm so tired of seeing nonalcoholic drinks in clunky pint glasses, this babe goes in a coupe. You can feel just as chic as your friends who are imbibing.

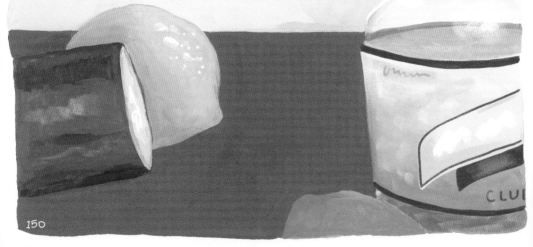

5 cucumber slices

Big handful of mint leaves

1 ounce simple syrup (page 162)

½ ounce lemon juice

½ ounce lime juice

Seltzer, to top

1 mint leaf, for garnish

Muddle the cucumbers, mint, and simple syrup in the bottom of a shaker tin. Add the lemon and lime juices and fill the shaker with ice. Shake until chilled, then double-strain into a coupe glass. Top with seltzer, garnish with a mint leaf, and serve.

VARIATION

Make It Your Major!: Add 1½ ounces white rum to the recipe and make it the same way. No need for seltzer.

1½ ounces sweet vermouth
1 ounce oloroso sherry
½ ounce Manzanilla sherry
3 dashes Angostura bitters
Seltzer, to top
1 lemon twist, for garnish

Combine all
ingredients
except the
seltzer and garnish
in an ice-filled Collins glass and stir
until chilled. Top with seltzer, garnish
with the lemon twist, and serve.

Aphrodite

At Sweet Polly, we had several cocktails on tap, and I was looking to add a low-ABV option. Sherry is a great base for this kind of drink since it's relatively low proof but still super flavorful. So I decided to take the Americano (page 50), an Italian combo of vermouth, Campari, seltzer, and ice, on a weekend trip to Spain. I swapped in two types of sherry for the Campari and added a touch of bitters. Simple yet delish. One of my friends described this drink as a "rich person's soda." Obsessed.

Fox Hollow

My dad's favorite drink was a Greyhound, otherwise known as a Vodka Grapefruit. He passed away when I was 15, so he never got to try one of my cocktails. The Fox Hollow is not only an homage to him and the summers we had together in our Long Island house on Fox Hollow Drive but also to the drinks we could have shared. This is what I would make for him if he could pull up a stool at my bar today.

The sugar on the rim of the glass evokes the sprinkle of sugar on brûléed grapefruits served at many classic diners, my dad's preferred kind of restaurant. The strawberry Campari goes beautifully with the natural bitterness of the grapefruit, and the lime juice, agave, and seltzer give it some Paloma (page 67) vibes, the ultimate drink of summer.

Citrus wedge, to rim the glass (optional)

Granulated sugar, to rim the glass

1½ ounces vodka

¾ ounce grapefruit juice

½ ounce lime juice

½ ounce Strawberry Campari (page 165)

½ ounce agave syrup (page 163)

Seltzer, to top

1 grapefruit twist, for garnish

Wet the side of a Collins glass with a citrus wedge or water, then roll the rim in sugar and fill the glass with ice. Combine all the remaining ingredients, except for the seltzer and garnish, in a shaker tin with a few cubes of ice. Shake until chilled, then strain into the prepared glass. Top with seltzer, garnish with the grapefruit twist, and serve.

1¾ ounces aged rum
¾ ounce sweet vermouth
½ ounce cinnamon syrup (page 163)
½ ounce Campari
Barspoon of cold-brew coffee
3 dashes molé bitters
1 orange twist, for garnish

Combine all the ingredients except for the garnish in a mixing glass filled with ice.

Stir until chilled, then strain into a Nick and Nora glass. Garnish with the orange twist and serve.

ALL-NIGHTER

At the end of a long, exhausting shift at the bar, my manager wanted a drink as I was closing up. I asked how she was feeling; she said (and I quote), "Cozy yet destructive." So I threw something together, handed it to her, and got back to closing. She took one sip and said that it needed to go on the menu. Problem was, I had no idea what I had made. The next two hours were spent trying to remember what I did, with my manager as the judge and jury. Was it ¼ ounce or ½ of Campari? Did I add the same amounts of cinnamon syrup and cold brew? How many dashes of molé bitters? Our 2 a.m. R&D session resulted in this spirit-forward, rum-based Negroni (page 51) variation that tastes kind of like dipping a Christmas cookie in coffee. I used Santa Teresa 1796, a rum aged in bourbon oak barrels, giving off vanilla and dark chocolate notes that go well with the cinnamon syrup and cold brew. But you can use any aged rum you'd like.

Sunset Sangria

For many summers now, my go-to concoction has been peach sangria. I whip it up for family and friends, and there's always a pitcher in the fridge, at the ready. It's a super-simple recipe of peaches soaked in peach brandy, some sort of light white wine, and peach seltzer (I like Polar's Georgia Peach seltzer). Easy and delicious, it's a real crowd-pleaser.

But the fun doesn't have to end when summer does. This is an updated version of that much-requested sangria, with fresh apples and apple brandy to welcome the fall. (Calvados is the apple brandy of choice here, since American apple brandy would be way too intense.) Instead of white wine, I love using rosé; it adds an extra level of flavor and lets me hold on to the last moments of summer. You can use a still or sparkling rosé, just make sure it's something you like to drink! (No need to go for anything expensive; sangria's a very forgiving gal.)

1 peach, pitted but unpeeled, finely chopped
1 apple, cored but unpeeled, finely chopped
1 cup (8 ounces) Calvados
½ cup (4 ounces) peach liqueur
1 (750ml) bottle of rosé, sparkling or still
1 can (12 ounces) peach seltzer

In a pitcher, combine the peach, apple, Calvados, and peach liqueur. Cover and let sit in the fridge for at least 30 minutes and up to 5 hours.
Add the rosé and seltzer, give it a stir, then cover and let sit in fridge for 1 hour.

To serve, pour into rocks glasses, with or without ice.

Bartending
Index

SYRUPS

SIMPLE SYRUP
Makes about 1½ cups

1 cup water
1 cup granulated sugar

Combine the water and sugar in a saucepan and bring to a simmer over low heat. Stir until the sugar fully dissolves.

DEMERARA SYRUP
Makes about 1½ cups

1 cup water
1 cup demerara sugar

Combine the water and sugar in a saucepan and bring to a simmer over low heat. Stir until the sugar fully dissolves.

GINGER SYRUP
Makes about 1 cup

1 (5-inch-long) piece fresh ginger (no need to peel)
1 cup demerara sugar

This one is a bit more involved but worth it. It's one part ginger juice to two parts demerara sugar, so make as much as you need. (If you don't have a juicer, you can find fresh ginger juice at some specialty stores; just make sure it's unsweetened.) Juice enough ginger to yield ½ cup, then fine-strain it. Combine the juice and sugar in a saucepan over low heat and bring to a very gentle simmer. Stir until the sugar fully dissolves.

CINNAMON SYRUP

Makes about 1½ cups

Handful of cinnamon sticks (about 4)
1 cup water
1 cup demerara sugar

Using a muddler or a wooden spoon, gently crush the cinnamon in a heavy-bottomed pot. Add the water and bring to a brisk simmer over low heat. Add the sugar and stir until the sugar fully dissolves. Once the sugar is fully dissolved, lower the heat and let simmer for about 30 minutes. Remove from the heat and fine-strain.

HONEY SYRUP

Makes about 1 cup

½ cup hot water
½ cup honey

Combine the honey and hot water in a heat-safe container and whisk until combined.

AGAVE SYRUP

Makes about 1 cup

½ cup hot water
½ cup agave nectar

Combine the agave nectar and hot water in a heat-safe container and whisk until combined.

RASPBERRY SYRUP

Makes about 1 cup

1 pint (2 cups) raspberries
¾ cup simple syrup

Combine the raspberries and simple syrup in a blender and blend until very smooth, 3 to 5 minutes. No need to strain.

KIWI HONEY

Makes about 1 cup

3 kiwis, peeled and chopped
¾ cup honey syrup

Combine the kiwis and honey syrup in a blender and blend until very smooth, 3 to 5 minutes. No need to strain.

Allow all syrups to cool before storing them in an airtight container in the fridge. Each should keep for up to 3 weeks.

Syrup made 3/23

Always label your syrups!

Infusions

All of these will theoretically last indefinitely.
But when in doubt, sniff it. The nose knows.

STRAWBERRY CAMPARI

Makes about 2 cups

1 pint (2½ cups)
strawberries,
hulled and sliced
2 cups Campari

Combine the strawberries
and Campari in
a food-safe
container. Put in
the fridge and let
sit for 2 to 3 days.
Fine-strain, then
store in the fridge.

ROSEMARY TINCTURE

Makes about ½ cup

½ cup fresh
rosemary leaves
½ cup vodka

Combine the rosemary
and vodka in a small,
airtight jar. Let sit
at room temperature
for up to 1 week,
agitating once a day,
then fine-strain. No
need to refrigerate.

EARL GREY VODKA

Makes about 1 cup

3 Earl Grey tea bags
(I like Twinings®)
1 cup vodka

Combine the tea bags and vodka in a jar with a lid. Let sit
for up to 1 hour, tasting every 10 minutes or so until it tastes
strongly of Earl Grey tea. Remove the tea bags and fine-strain.
Store in the fridge.

COCONUT-WASHED BAIJIU

Makes about 1¼ cups

1½ cups baijiu
8 tablespoons melted coconut oil

Combine the baijiu and coconut oil in a food-safe, freezer-safe container. Whisk to combine, then let sit at room temperature for about 4 hours. Cover and place in the freezer overnight (about 10 hours). Lift off the frozen solid oil, then strain the liquid through a fine-mesh strainer or cheesecloth. Store in the fridge.

PECAN BOURBON

Makes about 1¼ cups

½ cup pecan halves
1½ cups bourbon

Preheat the oven to 400°F. Spread the pecans out on a baking sheet and toast for 5 minutes, moving them around a few times so they don't burn. Let cool completely. Combine the pecans and bourbon in an airtight jar. Let sit at room temperature for 2 to 3 days, then fine-strain. No need to refrigerate.

JALAPEÑO-INFUSED TEQUILA

Makes about 2 cups

2 large jalapeños, sliced
2 cups blanco tequila

Combine the jalapeños—seeds and all—and tequila in a food-safe container. Let sit for 30 minutes, tasting every 10 minutes until it's as spicy as you want. Fine-strain, then store in the fridge.

TOOLS

SHAKERS: for shaking drinks

TIN ON TIN: two stainless steel tins

BOSTON SHAKER: one tin, one pint glass

COBBLER SHAKER: the three-piece-suit of shakers

LITERALLY ANYTHING WITH A LID: a food-safe container, Mason jar, blender bottle, quart container; if you can shake it and it has a lid, it'll work.

STRAINERS: for straining drinks

HAWTHORNE STRAINER: for straining shaken drinks, use with a shaker tin

JULEP STRAINER: for straining stirred drinks, use with a mixing glass

FINE STRAINER / CONE STRAINER: for double-straining drinks

ANYTHING THAT HOLDS BACK ICE: a slotted spoon, a storage container lid, another glass, a coffee filter if you have the patience of a saint.

MIXING GLASSES:
for stirring drinks

PINT GLASS: the tapered shape makes stirring easier

YARAI GLASS: stunning and elegant with a convenient spout

LITERALLY ANY GLASS: It'll get the job done as long as it can hold the liquid and ice.

JIGGERS: for
measuring all liquids

LEOPOLD: bell-shaped

JAPANESE-STYLE: tall and sleek

OXO GOOD GRIPS mini angled measuring cup

TABLESPOONS: One tablespoon equals a half ounce, so if push comes to shove and you need to do math, there it is.

SPOONS: for
stirring drinks

BARSPOON: good for stirring drinks in a mixing glass.

TEARDROP SPOON: good for stirring drinks built over a big ice cube.

ANYTHING THAT CAN STIR: It's not rocket science. Do you have a regular spoon or a chopstick or a knife or a clean finger? You can stir a cocktail.

MUDDLERS: for breaking up and muddling herbs, fruit and sugar cubes

WOODEN: cute, quaint, and easily stained

PLASTIC: chunky, indestructible, and awesome

ANYTHING THAT CAN SMASH STUFF: a wooden spoon, a potato masher, anything that's kind of heavy that you don't really care about.

JUICER: for . . . juicing

HANDHELD: the easiest and simplest way to go

CITRUS PRESS: If you're really into making shaken drinks at home, this would be worth getting.

YOUR OWN TWO HANDS: Crush that lemon like the Hulk!

PEELER: for making citrus peels

Y-PEELER: Yes, the veggie peeler. This is the only tool you should use, but I guess you could use a paring knife if you need to.

SHAKING

REGULAR/HARD SHAKE:

First, add all your ingredients to one of your shaker tins and fill it with ice. Place the other tin, bottom up, over the tin holding the ingredients and give it a good smack to create a firm seal. Shake vigorously for 10 to 20 seconds, until the tins get nice and frosty. A bartender's shaking style is a personal choice and takes time to develop; there's no "right way" to shake. When you're done, whack the side of the tin near the seal to release, making sure all your ingredients are in the bottom tin.

DRY SHAKE:

This means shaking without ice. It's done with egg white cocktails in order to emulsify and build up the proteins to get the cocktail nice and frothy. Shake your cocktail without ice for 10 to 20 seconds, then check the tin to make sure the mixture is foamy. Add ice and shake vigorously for 10 to 20 seconds. This dilutes and chills your cocktail. Always double-strain (page 172) when using egg whites.

Clearly not a dry shake

STIRRING

Add all your ingredients to your mixing glass, then add ice. Dunk your barspoon to the bottom of the glass, press the back of the spoon against the side, and gently rotate it around the glass. It takes a while to get the hang of this. Don't bob it up and down like a paintbrush—you want to eliminate air bubbles, not make them. Stir for 20 to 30 seconds, until the glass is good and cold.

BUILDING

This just means adding all your ingredients directly to your drinking vessel.

Mixing glass and dog not to scale

MUDDLING

This is the act of breaking up a fresh ingredient to release its oils or juices. Basically, you mash the ingredients in the tin or glass with a muddler. If a drink requires something to be muddled, do it first, before you add the other ingredients. Muddle fruit, veggies, or sugar cubes firmly in order to crush them. Muddle herbs a little more gently, so as not to bruise them and make them bitter. It helps to muddle herbs along with the syrup you're using, to soften the blow a bit.

DOUBLE-STRAINING

Use this technique when you want to smooth out your cocktail, ridding it of any ice chips or bits of muddled fruit. Put the Hawthorne strainer on top of your tin. Use your non-pouring hand to hold the cone strainer over your glass, then pour the liquid through the strainers into the glass.

RINSING

A rinse imparts the taste and aroma of an aggressively flavored spirit, liqueur, or tincture to your cocktail, without overpowering the drink. Add a small amount of the rinse ingredient into your glass. Swirl it around a few times so it coats the inside of the glass, then dump it out. You can also put whatever it is into a little spray bottle and give the glass a good spritz or two.

RIMMING A GLASS

This is usually done with salt or sugar and must be done before straining your cocktail. First, wet the outside of the glass with water or a citrus wedge. Then roll the outer rim of the glass in the substance; the liquid holds on to the salt or sugar and keeps it from falling into the drink. (If a bartender does this incorrectly and just dunks the glass straight into the salt, your Margarita will be unbearably salty when you're almost finished.)

COUPE

This can be used for any drink served up (without ice). I tend to use these for shaken drinks and Nick and Nora glasses for stirred drinks, but really, you can use the two glasses interchangeably. Rumor has it that the first coupe was shaped to resemble Marie Antoinette's boob. (That is my favorite bartending fun fact, regardless of whether or not it's true.)

NICK AND NORA

These feel super elegant and I'll drink anything out of one. It's my choice vessel for stirred drinks, far preferred over those giant V-shaped Martini glasses, which, to me, are slosh-city.

COLLINS

Use this sucker for two-ingredient highballs (Vodka Soda, Gin and Tonic, etc.) as well as any drink topped with seltzer.

173

ROCKS

Use these for serving spirits neat or on the rocks (hence, a rocks glass), or for any drink served over ice. Bigger ones, also called double rocks glasses or Old Fashioned glasses, will accommodate more ice and larger drinks, as well as those gorgeous big ice cubes.

FLUTE

This is the perfect shape for bubbles or cocktails that are mostly bubbles, like the French 75 (page 59).

MULE MUG

Traditionally for Moscow Mules (page 75), though you can put anything in these copper mugs, this goes best with drinks served over crushed ice.

WINE GLASS

Use this for higher-volume drinks served over ice (like spritzes). The stem is useful so your hand doesn't warm the drink.

JULEP CUP

A gorgeous jewel of a cup that you can use for any cocktail served over crushed ice, it's also the most stolen glass from any bar. (Please don't steal them.)

MASON JAR

It's a glass in my house—don't judge me. I use it for drinks served long, like Palomas (page 67), or refreshing cocktails served over ice, like Margaritas (page 64)—but also for any drink when all my other glasses are dirty.

GARNISHES

My philosophy about garnishes is that they should be aesthetically pleasing, yes, but always functional. A garnish should add something to the drink, not be a distraction. No need to put a hat on a hat.

TWISTS:

Pieces of citrus peel about 1 inch wide and 4 inches long. Take a Y-peeler diagonally across the fruit to get the best-size peel, and be careful about getting too much of the white pith, as it's super bitter. (Don't use a channel knife—we're not going for those slinky-like citrus twists of the 1990s.) After cutting the citrus for your garnish, express the citrus oils over your cocktail: hold the peel with the pith side facing you, then squeeze it over the top of the glass. You can twist the peel and lay it on the rim of the glass, or you can drop it right in if you want it to continue flavoring your cocktail. Or discard it all together if you just want the oils.

CITRUS WEDGES:

Great for Collins-style drinks or shaken drinks served on the rocks to add a bit more tartness as you go. Hot take: I really despise putting wedges on the rim of coupe glasses. It looks so awkward, and if it falls in, it feels like you're bobbing for apples. I much prefer citrus wheels (see next page).

CITRUS HALF-MOONS:

This is your best option for larger fruit like oranges and grapefruits, because a wheel of a grapefruit would take up your entire glass. To make a half-moon, just cut a citrus wheel in half. These can also be skewered on a cocktail pick or, if your cocktail is served over ice, dropped right in the glass.

CITRUS WHEELS:

A fragrant garnish that can either go on a pick, float on top of the surface of the cocktail, or, when notched, sit on the rim of the glass. (A wheel on the rim looks cute; a wedge, not so much.) Cut a lemon or lime into roughly $\frac{1}{8}$-inch crosswise slices.

HERBS:

Fresh herbs can really enhance the aromatics of a cocktail. Place the herbs in the palm of your hand and smack 'em before adding to the tin or garnishing your drink. It helps release their oils and also your anger!

A mint bouquet is a bunch of sprigs together used for garnish (like a bouquet of flowers!). Grab a bushy bundle of mint sprigs and remove any leaves from the middle and bottom of the stems, leaving the crowns intact. Smack the bouquet against your palm to release the oils, then nestle it right by the straw so you get the delicious scent each time you take a sip. Makes a world of difference.

OLIVES/ CHERRIES/ BERRIES:

Skewer these on a cocktail pick. I love green Castelvetrano olives for Martinis (page 46), Luxardo brandied cherries for Manhattans (page 49), and fresh blackberries or raspberries for pretty much anything.

STRAWS: Use metal instead of plastic! Save the turtles!

ICE

Ice is the secret weapon in all cocktails. It dilutes them but also brings them to the right temperature, which is cold. No one likes a lukewarm cocktail. For shaken drinks, ice also plays a crucial role in agitating the ingredients to create that lovely foam on top.

Choice of ice for each drink is also important to think about: Do you want the cocktail to continue to dilute as you drink it? If yes, serve it on the rocks. Or do you want to control the amount of dilution and have it remain constant while you sip the drink? In that case, serve it up. Do you want it to dilute slowly (use a big cube) or a little faster (use smaller cubes)? These minutiae matter!

ONE-INCH CUBES:

Use these cubes for shaking and stirring and in drinks served in Collins and rocks glasses. Buy a silicone mold for perfect 1-inch-square cubes.

BIG CUBES:

Two-inch square ice cubes look super sleek in an Old Fashioned (page 45) or other stirred cocktails, as well as some shaken ones, served in a rocks glass. You can also get silicone molds for these.

179

SPHERES:

Beautifully round ice spheres have less surface area than similarly sized cubes, so they dilute even slower. Olivia has a sphere mold that looks like the Death Star that she won in a game of White Elephant!

CRUSHED ICE:

Also called pebble or pellet ice, this is ice that, for home-bartending purposes, is literally crushed. Seriously, just put some ice cubes in a zip-lock bag and crush 'em. Great for refreshing drinks like a Mint Julep (page 80) or tropical drinks like a Piña Colada (page 96).

FREEZER ICE:

If you only have those cloudy, flimsy ice cubes that your freezer spits out, you can still make cocktails! These will dilute a lot faster than nicer cubes, so load up your shaker or mixing glass and just shake or stir for less time than you might otherwise.

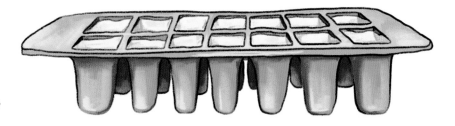

Ice, sometimes okay for snacking

Essential Shopping Lists

I love a good list. Here are two lists of the basics you'll need in order to make delicious drinks at home.

Necessary grocery items for great at-home cocktails:

- White granulated sugar
- Honey
- Lemons
- Limes
- Oranges
- Seltzer
- Green olives
  (if you're a Martini person)
- Brandied cherries
  (if you're a Manhattan person)

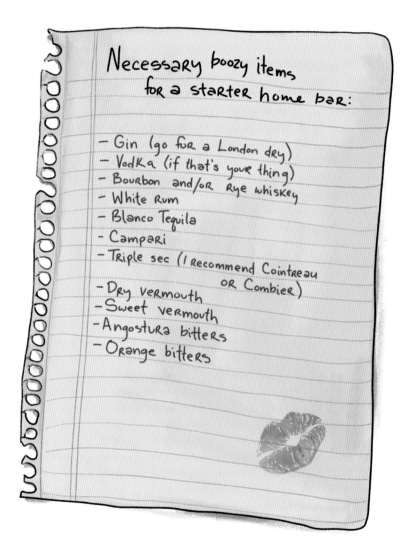

Necessary boozy items
   for a starter home bar:

— Gin (go for a London dry)
— Vodka (if that's your thing)
— Bourbon and/or Rye whiskey
— White Rum
— Blanco Tequila
— Campari
— Triple sec (I recommend Cointreau
                or Combier)
— Dry vermouth
— Sweet vermouth
— Angostura bitters
— Orange bitters

Acknowledgments

First and foremost we have to thank the incredible crew at Union Square & Co.: Amanda Englander, Caroline Hughes, Melissa Farris, Scott Amerman, Kevin Iwano, and everyone else who made this dream of ours into a reality. None of this would have been possible without Jennifer Williams; we are so appreciative that you brought us into the fold.

Huge thank-you goes to our editor, Emily Timberlake. Your input and advice have been invaluable, and we are so lucky to have had the opportunity to work with you.

Jenny Stephens, our agent at Sterling Lord Literistic. Thank you so much for taking a chance on us and believing in our work.

From Sammi

Mom. My best friend, my cheerleader, my hero. Thank you for being the most supportive, wonderful parent anyone could ask for. And yes, I know, you always said I was going to be a writer. You were right. I love you to the moon.

Aunt Pam, my introduction to food and drink. Thank you for always remembering to bring the Aperol.

My therapist. I guarantee I wouldn't have made the leap into cocktail writing without you. I am forever grateful.

Noah. Thank you for encouraging me to get back into bartending, for giving me a proper office setup, for loving and supporting me throughout all of it.

Peter, for passing me the head bartender torch and answering my bewildering texts in the midnight hour. I learned from the best.

Tom, my ride-or-die, my work husband. Thank you for always being by my side and for handing me a shot of Monte when you know I need it.

An enormous thank-you to Murat, AnnaGrace, Jeanette, and the entire team at Sweet Polly for always having my back.

All of my friends who have been there for me and encouraged me to go down this path: Nora, Kemba, Melanie, Austin, Sterling, Robert, Kaitlin, Alex, Jack, Elise, Adam, Liv, Sophie, Jess, Travis, Sam, and Lizzie. I'm so incredibly lucky to have you all in my corner.

My family for their endless love and support: David, Nancy, Lizanne, Samy, Gracie, Clara, Jesse, Alison, and Madison.

Thank you to all my dudes at Bathtub Gin who saw something in me that I didn't know was there. Thank you to every teacher who emboldened my creativity. Thank you to all of the cocktail writers and cocktail bars that have inspired me.

And lastly, to Olivia. You are the best friend, creative partner, taste-tester, and artist I could ever imagine. I could fill another book with how grateful I am for you and how much I love you. Cheers to many more.

From Olivia

Zach, thank you for being the best a gal could ask for. Truly none of this would have been possible without you. Sorry about all those nights and weekends I put myself in Painting Jail! I love you. Tom Collins on me for life.

Rebecca and Leah for your eternal cheerleading and cheers-ing. Lizzie, Caroline, Timb, Nora, Nadja—I am immensely lucky to have friends such as you.

Deep appreciation to my Harper community, and Jo especially for looking over early drafts of fonts and layouts.

Mom, Dad, Aidan, Liza—It is rare when your creative family is also your blood family. You all have taught me what it looks like to live as an artist, and what it means to gather with loved ones around good food and drink. *Saluti!*

Samwise, I love ewe. Ours is one of my most cherished partnerships, in work and play alike. *CinCin* to you always.

Index

U

UNION
SQUARE
& CO.

NEW YORK

ISBN 978-1-4549-4444-7

Library of Congress Cataloging-in-Publication Data:
Names: Katz, Sammi, author. | McGiff, Olivia, author.
Title: Cocktails in color : a spirited guide to the art and joy of
    drinkmaking / Sammi Katz & Olivia McGiff.
Description: New York : Union Square & Co., [2022] | Includes index. |
    Summary: "A guide to the elements, tastes, and techniques of
    drinkmaking. Featured are recipes for classic and original cocktails, as
    well as a Bartending Index, including additional recipes, tools and
    techniques, glassware and garnishes, and ice. Each page is illustrated
    with gouache paintings"-- Provided by publisher.
Identifiers: LCCN 2022008489 | ISBN 9781454944447 (hardcover) | ISBN
    9781454944454 (epub)
Subjects: LCSH: Cocktails. | BISAC: COOKING / Beverages / Alcoholic /
    Bartending & Cocktails | COOKING / Beverages / Alcoholic / Spirits |
    LCGFT: Cookbooks.
Classification: LCC TX951 .K27 2022 | DDC 641.87/4--dc23/eng/20220318
LC record available at https://lccn.loc.gov/2022008489

For information about custom editions, special sales, and premium purchases, please contact specialsales@unionsquareandco.com.

Printed in China

2 4 6 8 10 9 7 5 3

unionsquareandco.com

Interior design and illustrations by Olivia McGiff

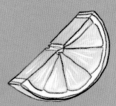